WE CAN'T ALL BE ASTRONAUTS

101 Ways to Survive Working for the Man

Michael Steadman

Dedicated to everyone running on the hamster wheel.
I know your legs are tired.

WE CAN'T ALL BE ASTRONAUTS
101 Ways to Survive Working for the Man

Copyright ©2026 by Michael Steadman
All rights reserved. No portion of this book may be reproduced in any form
without written permission from the author, except as permitted by U.S. copyright law.

Connect with the author at OfficeAstronaut.com
ISBN 979-8-218-79928-1
First edition: February 2026

WHAT PEOPLE MIGHT BE SAYING

"I don't know. What do you want me to say? I guess some parts are kind of funny." – Wife

"If he sells any books, I'm definitely asking for a trampoline and new soccer cleats." – Son

"You do realize AI could have written this in five minutes." – Former friend

Yes, it would be better to have actual quotes, preferably accolades from a respected book reviewer or celebrity. If anyone fitting that description wants to do me a solid, feel free to say something along the lines of: "Most important book since the Bible!" I don't want to put words in your mouth. You can gush any way you see fit and I'll work it into future printings of the book.

Thank you.

CONTENTS

Preface .... *i*

MAKE WORK SUCK LESS

Cope

Blame NASA 3
Make Mornings Suck Less (Step I) 4
Make Mornings Suck Less (Step II) 6
Look Forward to Something 8
Call the Police, PowerPoint Is Trying to Kill You 10
Emulate the Duck 12
Savor Shunky Time 14
Screw Commuting 15
Feast in Your Ford 16
Drink Good Coffee 18
Celebrate Life's Number Twos 20
Use Your Words 22
Get Some Help 24
FART 25
Find a Mentor 27
Flee Toxic People 29
Fake It 'til You Make It 31
Spruce Up That Carpeted Jail Cell 32
Steer Clear of Vending Machines 34
Remember, You're the Real Rock Star 36

Succeed

Settle Down Hot Shot 39
Make Yourself Comfortable 41
Be Pseudo Indispensable 43
Grin and Bear It 45
Watch Out for Shrapnel 46

Beware the Corporate Wedgie 48
Step It Up Slacker 50
Communicate Like a Pro 52
Add Random Letters After Your Name 54
Sport Some Specs 56
Wait Here Personal Problems 57
Stop Being a Jackass (or an Elephant) 58
Make Your Math Teacher Proud 60
Scribble on Your White Board 61
Dress Shabbily 63
Quit Staring at Your Shoes 65
Change Your Name to Doctor Bullshit 67
Show Up 69
Circle Back and Kiss My Ass 70
Put 'er There 72
Embrace Shortcuts 73
Be Tenacious 74

Play Nicely with Others

Stop Being Petty 76
Lighten Up, for the Love of God 78
Win Friends with Chocolate 80
Go on Mute Genius 82
Dial Up the Crazy 83
Show Some Respect 85
Pat Someone on the Back 86
Pee Silently 87
Learn from Art the Fart 89
Be Young and Good Looking 91
Pucker Up Baby 93
Quit Your Whining 95

CONTENTS

Mind Your Microwave Manners 97
Stop Eating Shit Sandwiches 99
Stay Away from Other People's Lunches 100
Eat the Breath Mint 101
Take Your Phlegm Elsewhere 103
Practice Prepathy 104
Cozy Up to a Colleague 105
Give in to Your Hero Cravings 107
Stop Acting Like a Smacked Ass 109
Cure That Diarrhea of the Mouth 111
Listen Up 113
Put the Dumb Smartphone Down 115
Curb "Reply to All" 117

Keep Yourself Amused

Stick to Non-mandated Fun 120
Milk the Baby 121
Play "Leave It and They Will Come" 122
Have a Joke Handy 124
Acquire Some Fake Vomit 125
Act Childish 127
Learn to Juggle 129
Find Time for a Field Trip 131
Make It Better with Bacon 133
Create a Fun Work Slogan 134
Pump Up the Volume 135
Enjoy Websites Sans Naked People 136
Celebrate Bogus Holidays 138
Act Offended 140
Take the Scenic Route 142

Stay Healthy

Abstain from Expiring at Work 144
Breathe Some Fresh Air 146
Stand up. 147
Don't Pull a Hammy 149
Choke Down Some Salad. 151
Sit Within Three Feet of an Exit. 153
Don't Stab Yourself with a Pencil 154
Don't Stab Someone Else with a Pencil. 156
Don't Get Stabbed by a Pencil 158

Out Of This World Free Time

Help a Brother Out 160
Consume Frosty Ale. 161
Get a Canine Companion 163
Visit the Dentist. 165
Watch the Best Work Movie Ever. 167
Hug Your Bad Habit 169
Go Away 171
Reform Your No-Good Ingrate Ways 173
Don't Be a Financial Fuckup 174
Sleep It Off 176
Let's Wrap This Up Already 178

"The beatings will continue until morale improves."

– Tee-shirt I bought at the Pirates of the Caribbean gift shop in Disney World

PREFACE

When writing a book, I've heard it's a good idea to have a point. You're in luck. I have two.

First and foremost, you possess money and I'd enjoy getting my hands on some of it. Writing a book allows me to do that, assuming I can dupe you into buying a copy.

I'm under no delusion that this book will rocket me into the orbit (puns intended) of never having to worry about money. Nonetheless, even a little income could help me move toward the ultimate goal—emancipation from working for the man.

Before setting out to write a book, I pondered other ways to make extra money. However, I've decided authoring a book is my best option.

For starters, I don't hate writing and I think I'm halfway decent at it. Plus, writing a book is legal.

That last point cannot be overemphasized because I wouldn't fare well in prison. I'm not sure I'd even survive the white-collar kind where inmates remain incarcerated by resisting the urge to drop their tennis rackets and jump over the shrubbery enclosures.

Plus, writing is easier than trying to start a company or invent something, like a new fruit-tea beverage or a smartphone for dogs. Those pursuits would be far too taxing for yours truly.

But enough about me. Let's focus on you, the reader. Right now, you're thinking: "Hey Mike. You're obviously a cool dude, but why should I read your dumb book?"

Well, thank you, and you're right. I am cool.

As far as your question, it's a good one, and I'm only partly saying this to butter you up. My answer to you is twofold. First and foremost, you should read my book for shits and giggles. You know, for laughs.

On top of amusement value, I believe my book offers some bono fide wisdom about making the most of your daily grind. It's wisdom I've acquired from schlepping to work for more years than I care to think about.

Not that you asked, but those are my motives for writing this book.

Before I go any further, I feel compelled to disclose a list of things this book won't do for you. This book won't make you slimmer, taller, more flexible, younger, smarter, richer, a better dancer, a better cook, bilingual, a better parent, better smelling, better in bed, more interesting, more energetic, more athletic, and it won't remove unsightly nose hair or excessive ear wax.

Furthermore, this book is not going to impress any snooty literary types, should you have any friends or family who fit that description. In fact, if such a person shows up on your doorstep looking for some wine and brie, I advise you to hide this sham of a book under the nearest sofa cushion.

Once your home is clear of the aforementioned literati, you can safely proceed with reading. By the time you're finished, you'll have learned how to:

- Curb homicidal tendencies at work.

- Avoid promotions.

- Make the most of toilet time.

- Slack off like a pro.

- Master the art of zoning out.

- And much, much more!

To oblige my more remedial readers, I've also thoughtfully divided this book into 101 simple actions even a dyslexic goldfish could follow.

This should come as welcome news if the next book you read will be your first. If that sounds like you, you've chosen wisely. You and your attention-deficit mind can relax because all you have to do is focus on the tips that interest you most. Jump around as much as you like.

Before I end this superb preface, I must stress how essential your financial support is. So, for the love of God, loosen the death grip on your wallet and buy a copy of this delightful book. It also wouldn't kill you to buy an extra copy—or 100—for friends, family, and total strangers.

100% NO MONEY-BACK GUARANTEE

Will you love my book? Damn straight! I guarantee it, although you mustn't interpret that as any kind of money-back guarantee.

While I can't stop you from returning the book for a refund, I implore you not to take such a drastic action. It would hurt my feelings. Rest assured, if I learn that you disliked my book, I'll experience genuine remorse, and those feelings could last as long as 3–4 minutes.

MAKE WORK SUCK LESS

DID YOU KNOW that "salary" comes from "salarium," the Latin word for salt? Yes, it's true. Why the hell would I make that up?

Before the Industrial Revolution, salt was in high demand. In fact, salt was such a valuable commodity people were sometimes paid with it.* On top of that, mining the stuff was dangerous, work often relegated to slaves and prisoners.

Well, I don't know about you, but I find this interesting. And that last factoid seems especially apropos for those of us who feel economically stuck toiling in a proverbial salt mine.

Never having met you, I don't know for sure exactly what's troubling you at work. Perhaps it's the stress or maybe it's the tight deadlines. Or maybe it's a co-worker with a severe flatulence problem. What I do know is that I can't focus on that right now.

What I would like to focus on in this part of the book is teaching you how to make your long hours on the hamster wheel less depleting.

To that end, I urge you to read on so that I may share my brilliance about how to bolster your happiness at work.

---

*Can you imagine? "Alright, thanks for all you did today, Jim. Enjoy this bag of salt. By the way, there's more where this came from, so be here tomorrow at 5 a.m. sharp."

WAYS TO COPE

Do you spend most of your workday in a fetal position under your desk whimpering like a scared puppy in a thunderstorm? Well, I'm no psychiatrist, but that's fucked up.

This first section of the book is designed to coax you out from under your desk. The first set of gems will help you cope more effectively with whatever your job dishes out.

Stellar Gem #1: Blame NASA

When you were a tyke, maybe you dreamed of becoming an astronaut or an NFL quarterback. Or maybe you wanted to be a mime. Really, how would I know?

The point is, life takes many of us down a path we never could have imagined. And while this isn't inherently bad, it can be a serious downer if you didn't wind up where you thought you'd be.

If you're in this camp, I can't bear to see you moping around. That's why I'm going to give you some helpful advice. If you find yourself in an undesirable career, remember—it's always best to blame others.

For example, let's say you desperately wanted to be an astronaut, but in reality, you're something much more mundane, like an accountant or a security guard at a yarn factory.

No problem. All you have to do is assume NASA lost your contact information. Bad break? You bet, but it's not your fault.

That's the beauty of my technique. Your dream employer simply should have been more careful with your resume. Careless bastards!

There are some people who may disagree with this approach. These people love to preach about "personal responsibility." Never listen to them. They're wrong and I'm right.*

Now, if I may, I'll wrap up with some perspective to further console you.

Riding a rocket to the space station or scoring the winning touchdown in a Super Bowl aren't the only ways to get an adrenaline rush. No sir.

For example, this week you and your co-workers might decide to mix things up and head out to Olive Garden for lunch instead of Applebee's.

Or who knows? Maybe when you get back from lunch, you'll discover some leftover birthday cake in the break room.

You see. Your life isn't sad and pathetic. Exciting possibilities abound.

---

*As a general rule, always assume I'm right. If this becomes difficult to remember, just say aloud this catchy phrase I've created to help you: "Mike's way is the right way."

Stellar Gem #2: Make Mornings Suck Less (Step I)

When you get to work in the morning and you're swearing like a sailor or openly weeping, you know you're in for a long day. Lucky for you, I have a simple two-step remedy. Smartly, I've decided to call them Step I and Step II.*

The first step is to address what may be happening (or not happening) before you arrive at work.

For many of us, mornings are chaotic. And it all starts horribly thanks to the most diabolical invention in human history—the alarm clock. After being jolted out of your peaceful slumber, the rat race is on, ready or not.

Rush, rush, rush . . . You frantically complete your rote morning rituals and make a mad dash for the office. Or, post-pandemic, maybe that's a mad dash to the laptop in your spare bedroom. Either way, it's downright uncivilized.

The answer, of course, is to get yourself out of bed earlier and start using your time more efficiently.

What's that? No, I will not go screw myself.

I know what I'm asking isn't easy. Waking up at the crack of dawn sucks. Yet if you give yourself a little extra time in the mornings it can make all the difference in how your day goes.

Easier said than done, yes, I know, but here are a few ideas to help you:

- **Sleep in your clothes.** If you're a parent or drunk a lot, you've probably done this. If you're hesitant to try this because you're worried about looking too wrinkled, please refer to Gem #35.

- **Eat breakfast in the shower.** I think I picked this idea up from a Seinfeld episode. Enjoy your Cocoa Pebbles in the shower and you can save precious minutes getting ready in the morning.

- **Slurp down coffee in your car.** But please don't be a moron. Severely burning one's crotch cannot put you on the path to a happier work life.** Avoid this unpleasant outcome by using some common sense. Refrain from trying to drink your brew until you hit a red light or when traffic comes to a grinding halt.

---

*I'm sure you'll agree that my choice to use of Roman numerals here clearly differentiates me as learned and extremely sophisticated. This knowledge should allow you to rest easy knowing that your purchase of my book was an extremely sound decision and a fine use of your hard-earned money.

**In the 1990s this happened to an elderly woman and she received close to $3 million from McDonald's in a lawsuit settlement. After her third-degree burns healed maybe she felt happier. I don't know, but best to keep hot beverages away from your crotch.

Stellar Gem #3: Make Mornings Suck Less (Step II)

Hopefully your brain has absorbed Step I because I'm moving on, with or without you. Yes, it's time to tackle the next step to making mornings suck less.

My second and final step is about fortune telling. No, this has nothing to do with a shady lady in a headscarf looking into a ball and filling your head with bunk predictions. Rather, it's about you attempting to be a fortune teller when it comes to predicting work is going to always suck. You've been bleakly prognosticating for far too long—and it's not helping, so stop telling yourself every day is going to be a crap storm full of calamities.

Is something crappy going to happen at work tomorrow that will send you into a fit of rage? Of course, you work in corporate America.

But something might go off without a hitch, or dare I say it, something might happen that brings a smile to your face. So why not focus on those possibilities?

Obsessing over what could go wrong during any given workday leads to nothing but a lifetime of misery. And what will your Woody Allen angst solve? Nada. All you'll succeed at doing is giving yourself an ulcer. Here's what to do instead:

1. **Strut around as much as possible.** I recommend a George Jefferson swagger. If you're too young to know who that is, go look it up. The swagger will speak volumes to your colleagues. It will say that you can't be flustered—and that you're not to be messed with under any circumstances.

2. **Redirect your negative energy.** This may sound like some serious hippie advice, but don't worry. It will work even if you don't smoke pot, have long hair, and sit cross-legged next to a mangy dog while chewing organic vegetables and strumming an acoustic guitar. Just find a better use for the energy you're currently wasting worrying. Do something more constructive, like solving world hunger or clipping your toenails.

3. **Take baby steps.*** No, please don't literally walk like a baby. That would be weird. Plus, when you consider how long it would take to get to your destination, it would be very impractical. Instead of being overwhelmed by your to-do list, simply chip away at it.

By the way, I've noticed a lot of people knocking the United States these days. Well, I'm here to say I don't like one bit. It upsets me greatly because I love my country.

Does the U.S. have its share of serious problems? Sure, poverty, crime, reality TV, synchronized swimming, and vegans, to name a few. But the last time I checked, the good old US of A is still a pretty darn great place to live and I personally feel blessed to be a citizen.

What does any of this have to do with Gem #3? I have no idea.

No, I'm kidding. I bring it up because I want you to be inspired by the long history of American optimism and carry on that proud tradition. Our optimism has been delusional at times, but I love how, generation after generation, our country has faced tough obstacles and somehow managed to overcome them.

Most of your problems are within your power to solve. You can do it!

---

*I can't tell you this and not think about by one of my favorite Bill Murray movies, "What about Bob?" Richard Dreyfuss plays a narcissistic psychiatrist who publishes a book called Baby Steps. If you've never seen it, do yourself a favor and watch it at once.

Stellar Gem #4: Look Forward to Something

Alright, tell me one thing you're really looking forward to at work tomorrow. Go ahead, lay it on me.

I'm waiting.

Uh-oh, can't do it?

Okay, settle down Chester. No need to get testy. If every day at work feels like an 8-hour root canal or being stuck in line at the DMV, I believe you. But it seems slightly unlikely that there aren't at least a few positive things that go on between the hours of 9 a.m. and 5 p.m.

Furthermore, I think if we put our heads together, we can come up with a short list of things you can look forward to. Once you nail that down, the next time you feel crappy at work, you'll be ready to do something about it. You'll focus your distressed brain on your list and voila—you'll start to feel more positive about your day.

Here are a few of mine you can use if you like:

- **Chow down.** Food is never a bad place to start and I bet you love nothing more than shoveling all manner of calories into your pie hole. It doesn't matter if you prefer caviar imported from Russia or beef jerky imported from your local convenience store. Food can make us happy.

- **Gaze upon something beautiful.** Maybe it's a hottie you sit next to. Maybe it's an amazing photo online. Maybe it's simply appreciating some nice landscaping outside your window. There's a lot of ugliness in the world, but there's also plenty of beauty if we notice it.

- **Ask a colleague a personal question.** If you're tired of work talk, you can always ask someone a question about themselves. This could lead to an interesting conversation. Even someone you're hesitant to talk to may have something captivating to say, maybe share something about an interesting hobby or how they wrestled an alligator or how they spend their spare time fighting crime.

Note: Please carefully consider your question. For example, "What are you most deeply ashamed of?" and "Have you always had a pungent body odor?" are not great conversation starters.

Let's see, what else? I feel like I'm forgetting something.

Eh, who cares? You have no way of knowing what I had in mind anyway, so you'll be none the wiser if I leave something out.

Stellar Gem #5: Call the Police, PowerPoint Is Trying to Kill You

The pyramids, Stonehenge, SPAM (the meat, not the email) . . . life is full of bona fide mysteries.

To me, the greatest mystery in the universe may be how so many corporate types have deluded themselves into believing you and I want nothing more than to listen to long-winded PowerPoint presentations full of mind-numbing numbers and charts.

Most corporate slide presentations are coma-inducing. Truth be told, their real "Power" is being boring, and that power is so potent it's responsible for the deaths of 26 office workers an hour in the United States.*

For those who routinely sit through presentations, you have my condolences. My recommendation is to take any and all measures to evade these life-depleting torture sessions. Feign illness, sit in the back of the room, sneak out when they dim the lights, send a look-a-like . . . whatever it takes. You don't deserve that kind of punishment.

As I see it, meetings deliver a one-two punch. First, there's a hard jab to the face. This takes the form of content dryer than the Sahara. Then there's the length, also known as the knock-out punch. There you sit, with dozens or even hundreds of others, held hostage until the speaker sees fit to dismiss you. And maybe the biggest kick in the pants—at least 99% of the time, the whole stupid thing could have been summed up in an email.

If you continue to be unlucky and can't avoid the darkness of meetings, it's critical to self-administer first aid once a meeting concludes. This is what I call the recovery phase. The recovery phase begins the second the presenter stops yammering. This is when you stand up to exit the room and discover you feel half dead.**

I have a lot of experience with the recovery phase. More times than I can count, I've had to revive myself by downing coffee, dousing myself with icy cold water, and throwing back some Tylenol. It's not pretty, but the recovery phase, if handled properly, will help you start to feel human again.

For those of you who hold court with a microphone, please wake up. I recognize that's vague advice, so let me be more specific. There are flaming red flags that are trying to tell you it's time for you to stop your yacking. Here are a few examples:

- Audience members are sound asleep as evidenced by closed eyes accompanied by significant snoring and drooling.

- While technically awake, many have entered a catatonic state.

- At least one person has a countenance resembling Edward Munch's famous painting *The Scream*.

- There's so much yawning all you can see are tonsils.

Jesus, at the very least, throw in a joke or two. Or pause and give people five or ten minutes to stretch and down some vodka. Better yet, forego the whole thing and let people go get some actual work done.

*Statistic may be bogus.

**Scratch that. You'll feel at least 97% dead.

Stellar Gem #6: Emulate the Duck

I have a confession, and I'm not going to lie to you, it's embarrassing.

I love ducks.

No, that's not a misprint.

Now the obvious question: Why?

Well, for starters, ducks are pretty darn cute, unlike those nasty, green-pooping Canadian geese that are so ubiquitous where I live.

I'm also fond of the saying "Let it roll off of you, like water off of a duck." I like this saying because it highlights one of the most valuable skills any of us can have at work, or anywhere else for that matter—resiliency.

There's no getting around it. Life is going to kick you in the nuts from time to time. And sometimes the kicker will be wearing steel-toed boots.

The good news is that once you can accept that disappointments are part of life, you don't have to allow them to totally wreck your life. You can control how they affect you.

Don't get me wrong. By all means, curse to your heart's content if it helps you feel better. Writhe around on the floor, groan, and curl up in a ball if you like. Just get back up and dust yourself off.

Winston Churchill said it best: "Never, never, never, never give up."*

I've certainly sustained my share of kicks. In my younger days, I didn't handle it well. Since then, I've developed thicker skin. Good for me.

When I became a dad, I began to prize resiliency even more. Upon learning I was going to be a dad my first thought was: "How am I going to take care of a baby? I can barely take care of myself!"

After my panic attack subsided, I started to think about other things, like: "What traits do I want to instill in my child?" Resiliency was right there at the top of the list.

If you're like me, you're not the smartest or most ambitious person in the room, but you don't need to be. You can still be successful if develop the ability to bounce back.

From now on, emulate the duck. And remember, no matter what—ducks will always be cuter than you.

---

*Another famous Churchill quote: "I may be drunk Miss, but in the morning, I will be sober, and you will still be ugly." It's simultaneously awful and funny, and quite ballsy coming from a guy who looked like a bulldog.

Stellar Gem #7: Savor Shunky Time

Sometimes you need a break, a break from work and, most importantly, a break from people.

I guess that's why we have vacation days. But what's a poor working stiff to do when those vacation days run out?

The answer is as close as the nearest restroom.

Maybe you've never thought of the bathroom as a sanctuary, or a place to seek rejuvenation, but I'm here to tell you—it is. The next time you're ready to blow a gasket at work, make a bee line for the shunky, which is a fun Scottish slang term for toilet.

The person who coined the name "restroom" was smart because the name is spot on. It's also a better name than "urine closet" or "room of foul-smelling odors."

Now let's delve a little deeper into the toilet.

To the unenlightened, the allure of a restroom is limited to the promise of relieving oneself. Philistines! That's like saying that he only purpose of food is to fill one's belly.

We should all venerate restrooms.

Why? Because toilets have stalls, and stalls offer the most coveted commodity in the modern workplace—doors!

In the 21st century, privacy at work has become as elusive as Sasquatch. The glorious restroom, however, remains a bastion of peace and tranquility.

And that's not all.

As an added bonus, you can elevate your restroom experience by closing your eyes when you flush. Listen to the flowing water and picture yourself sitting on a white sand beach watching foamy waves crash over the rocks of a tropical island. It's like a mini beach vacation and it won't cost you a nickel.*

---

*To take it up another notch, bring a can of Febreze. You'll be doing the next person a big favor and you can feel even more like you're reclining in the sands of Hawaii or Bora Bora. Yes, Febreze is available in both those scents. No, I have no idea if they are authentic or if there's really any difference between the two.

Stellar Gem #8: Screw Commuting

I don't know where you hang your hat, although you impress me as someone who'd wear a sombrero. Regardless of your questionable fashion choices, before you can hang that hat, you need to make your way home from work, provided the plague didn't send you into a permanent work from home gig. If you're still commuting to work, even some of the time, chances are that trip is not fun.

I live in the Philly area, and around here, we don't need traffic reports. Roads are always more clogged than the arteries of a 400-pound dude living on bacon double cheeseburgers and ice cream.

For a time, I drove an hour each way to work. For the math challenged, that comes out to a tragic waste of 10 hours of my life every week, or about 500 hours a year! Someone pass the Prozac.

I know what you're thinking. "Hey Mike, how about some cheese to go with that whine?" Well yes, I'd love some cheese, but don't change the subject.

Every hour you squander commuting is an hour of your life you'll never reclaim, and that's grim. The whole gigantic mess is why, when I bought my first home, I chose one located close to work. That cut my commute to a very manageable 10 minutes.

What about you?

If your drive is draining you, do something about it. Find some virtual work or rein in that commute by getting a hacienda closer to work.

Still not convinced?

Okay, try this. The next time you're traveling down the road at a snail's pace, think about the million more enjoyable things you could be doing.

Now go pack your bags, and good luck with the move.

Free moving tip: If you're in your 20s, your friends will help you move your worldly possessions in return for greasy pizza and beer. However, if you're over 30, hire a mover. Even if you somehow manage to lure your buds with suds and pizza, due to their advancing age, it will likely cause them considerable intestinal distress and they'll wake the next day crippled with back pain, cursing your name.

Stellar Gem #9: Feast in your Ford

It's a horrible idea to eat lunch at your desk. It's even worse when you're having an extra stressful day.

I understand why you break out your My Little Pony lunch pail at your desk when lunchtime rolls around. Maybe there are too many deadlines looming. Or some jerk roped you into an early afternoon meeting that makes it impossible for you to go out to eat with your chums.

I get it. Nevertheless, even when you're pressed for time, you still have to find a way to break away, even if it's only for 15 or 20 minutes.

Sure, there will be days when you need to stay close to the office, but you don't have to stay in the building. Grab your food and head for the parking lot. That's right, you'll be dining in your car.

If it's never occurred to you to eat lunch in your car, you've been missing out. Dining in your car is like having your very own mobile restaurant. It can be just what the doctor ordered when you're trying to power through a tough day.

The best part is it doesn't matter what kind of car you drive. To have an enjoyable lunch, you don't need heated seats or mahogany wood inlay.

Not sold on the idea?

Okay, let's look at the perks.

For starters, you can put the windows down if it's a beautiful day. Or you can crank up the air conditioner or heater if it's not a beautiful day. Then, once you've settled in, you can listen to that smooth jazz you love so much.

After you've swallowed the last tasty morsel, recline the seat, and take a quick nap to complete your rejuvenation. Then you'll be ready, or as ready as you can be, to face the afternoon crap storm.

In conclusion, I'll leave you with a quote from Tom Hodgkinson, author of *How to Be Idle*, a tremendously funny book that I highly recommend. This quote is from his chapter "The Death of Lunch":

> *"We need to claim lunch back. It is our natural right. It has been stolen from us by our rulers. The fear that keeps you chained to your desk, staring at your screen, does not serve your spirit. Lunch is a time to forget about being sensible, practical, and efficient. A proper lunch should be spiritually as well as physically nourishing."*

Amen Mr. Hodgkinson.

Stellar Gem #10: Drink Good Coffee

As a young lad, getting me to drink coffee was a herculean task. You would have had a better chance of getting me to drink paint thinner. Well, those days are over. Now, if I don't get my morning fix, I turn into the crotchety old man who yells at kids to get off his lawn.

Coffee has the power to jolt us back to life, and nothing smells better than fresh brewed coffee. Well, bacon smells better, but coffee is a close second.

If you don't drink coffee, shame on you. You should start immediately.

No, seriously. Go get a mug of it right now. I'll wait.

What's that? Oh please.

I don't want to hear about your heart palpitations or complaints that you don't like the taste. If you don't like the taste, you're simply not adding enough cream and sugar. Now put aside your lame excuses and get onboard the java train. You dig?

Next, I'd like to talk to you about coffee quality, but before I do, I apologize to those of you already regularly drinking coffee. I fear I've wasted your time. Please move on to my next gem.

As for the rest of you, fasten your seatbelts. Here are my enthralling coffee drinking insights . . .

First, always say no to free coffee. If your employer offers free coffee, run. That swill will taste like a mixture of gasoline and dirty bath water. True, it does contain the wonderful drug caffeine, but that doesn't begin to make up for the awful taste.

The great news is that you don't have to drain your wallet to enjoy an excellent cup of Joe. In fact, I believe a lot of the most expensive coffees are also the worst tasting.* Some of my favorite coffees are the most inexpensive brands on the shelf.

Now let's turn our attention to coffee grinding.

I'm busy. I don't have time to be grinding coffee beans. I do see the merits of it though. So, have at it if you want.

Finally, when I say "Enjoy good coffee" this also means savor it, like a civilized human being. Coffee is not meant to be guzzled like some knucklehead draining a keg at a frat party.

---

*For me, this also holds true for wine drinking. If you're a snooty wine connoisseur, you no doubt disagree with me, but I won't be swayed by the fact that I have an unsophisticated palette and you are much more knowledgeable. I'm not out to impress anyone. So, please leave me in peace to enjoy my $3 bottle of vino from the great wine region of North Dakota.

Stellar Gem #11: Celebrate Life's Number Twos

I love my dog Haley and I greatly miss my Lab mix, Murphy, who went to the big dog park in the sky.

Murphy was a great dog, but he was also a bit of a headcase.

Anyway, when I'd take my good buddy Murphy for a walk, he'd like to stop along the way to deposit a deuce and this was always followed by a tremendous display of celebration. The celebrating took the form of considerable grass kicking and tail wagging combined with some crazy running about. It was entertaining.

Sometimes I'd watch his antics and wonder: Does Murphy think he scored the winning touchdown in the Super Bowl? Or is he under the impression that he's been called up on stage to accept an Oscar for best dog actor? I'll never know.

You, however, are a person, not a dog. Or at least I assume that's true. As a human, I can only hope you're not defecating outside. If you are, I definitely don't want to hear about it.

Also, unless you're a total nut job, you don't see eliminating bodily waste as cause for rejoicing.

If you don't see where I'm going with all of this, that's understandable because I'm rambling. What I'm trying to say is that I believe my dog had an important lesson to teach us. Professor Murphy, by example, was telling me to celebrate even life's smallest accomplishments.

You can do it too. Allow me illustrate with a few examples.

Let's say the hot shot down the hall just landed a new multi-million-dollar client. Bully for him, but you've done cool stuff too.

For starters, you dragged your tired body out of bed this morning and managed to start work sort of on time. In my book, that's heroic. For sure, worthy of some self-congratulations. So, go ahead and give yourself a pat on the back.

Let's see, what else?

Hey, you frequently remember your user name and password. Congratulations, gold star!

Word at the water cooler is you also organized your paper clips recently. Amazing!

These are your number twos. Celebrate them!

The next time you're slogging through a workday, be mindful of the small accomplishments. More importantly, let them bring you joy, like man's best friend.

Stellar Gem #12: Use Your Words

There's a car in my neighborhood with a bumper sticker that reads "Running is cheaper than therapy."

I agree that exercise is an excellent way to decompress and that's important because too much stress will put you in the looney bin. I submit, however, that there is a better, free way to vent: Use your words.

At work, you might be tempted every 10 minutes or so to climb on top of your desk and unleash a torrent of obscenities. Or you might have a burning urge to put all the vitriol into an e-mail and send it to everyone at your company.

As amusing as that would be, I cannot endorse that sort of thing, unless you've truly had it and don't care if you get canned.

If you need a way to unburden your disturbed mind, one that won't get you fired, try writing down what's eating at you—but keep it to yourself.

"What is the point of that," you ask?

Because writing is cathartic, damn it. Now stop with your uppity questions!

Start thinking of something to write. Here are a couple of samples to get your creative juices flowing:

Memo

Dear Corporate Overlords:

This place sucked the life out of me faster than an industrial strength Hoover. You're the worst.

Kind regards,

[Your Name]

Diary entry

Dear Diary,

What a day. Here's a recap: 9 a.m. – team introduced to new co-worker, Drew; 9:05 a.m. everyone agrees Drew is a jerk and Joe suggested smothering him with a pillow; 10:23 – group concludes it would be wrong to murder Drew; 12 noon – ate something; 12:30 p.m. – headed to the lactation room for a well-deserved nap; 4 p.m. – woke from nap; 4:05 p.m., logged back on and pretended to work; 4:30, Couldn't take any more and went to the bar.

I hope you found those examples helpful.

No matter how badly you want to use a sword, remember the pen is mightier. Besides, you'd never get your commemorative *Game of Thrones* sword past security.

Stellar Gem #13: Get Some Help

One thing I learned in Catholic school was that God doesn't like pride. In fact, it made the "Seven Deadly Sins" list.

That's not to say pride is always a negative. Pride can motivate us to do our best. However, it can cause big problems, especially when Mount Everest-sized egos are involved.

One common example of pride getting ugly is when you're overwhelmed but won't admit it. You desperately need help, but you won't ask because you're afraid it will make you look weak and/or stupid.

If you are weak and/or stupid, that's fine. However, given you're reading this high-brow book, that can't possibly be the case.

Now, let's see. Where was I? Oh yes, now I remember.

If you're prideful and stubborn about seeking help, don't be. Check your ego at the door and raise your hand if you need help. This can be done in such a way that it won't lead your boss to conclude you have the IQ of a rock or the work ethic of a Basset Hound.

It's all about humility, which is tragically hard to find in corporate America.

The nuns at my elementary school were right. Pride really can lead us down a dark, "deadly" road.

Religion aside, if you're too proud to admit when you're in over your head, you're going to be crazy stressed. This will make your hair fall out and people will tease you and give you unfortunate nicknames, like cue ball. Then the stress will eventually kill you.

I don't want to see that happen because, truth be told, I've grown somewhat fond of you, so be humble and let someone know when you need help.

Stellar Gem #14: FART

I think we can all agree that acronyms are stupid. So, naturally, corporations can't get enough of them and my book wouldn't be complete without creating one of my own.

My new acronym is FART. Here's what it stands for:

Fans of
Acronyms
Ruin
Tuesdays and every other day

Kidding aside, acronym overuse makes people want to scream. It's beyond annoying and we must put a stop it. Who's with me?

Given how ubiquitous the problem is, I'm hazy on how to curb the problem. A good first step might be to lead by example. If we refrain from using acronyms, others may follow suit.

Idiotic abbreviations are deeply ingrained in work culture and the problem is compounded by the fact that people in business schools and office buildings around the country are constantly coming up with new ones. That's why the ultimate response has to be more drastic.

When I'm elected president, I'll institute reeducation work camps for offenders. My 12-week program will be headquartered somewhere remote, maybe Mongolia. During this time, offenders will relearn how to speak English. If, at the end of that time, a person cannot pass a final exam, repeating the program will be necessary.

Following are some examples from the exam:

Please select the appropriate acronym-free choice.	**Verbal reinforcement**
o Kindly stop harassing Greta ASAP.	Sorry, incorrect. You're a massive disappointment.
o Kindly stop harassing Greta as soon as possible.	Nice work!
o Tell the CEO he makes way too much money.	A thousand times no.
o Tell the chief executive officer he makes way too much money.	Superb!
o What kind of ROI can we expect?	Ugh.
o What kind of return on investment can we expect?	By George, you got it!

Until that's up and running, when you hear acronym abuse at work, sit the lad or lass down and have a heart-to-heart chat. Explain the offensive violation and how it's making the person sound like a dope.

Lastly, it's imperative for you to encourage others to aid you in policing this problem. You will need the patience of Job, but don't give up. You're doing yeoman's work and I'm depending on you.

Stellar Gem #15: Find a Mentor

I think we can all agree that Seinfeld was one of the best TV shows ever. Or maybe we can't. Who cares?

I love every episode of Seinfeld, except the final one. That was awful. One favorite episode is the one where Jerry is dating a girl who has a mentor.

Jerry, true to his shallow nature, ultimately breaks up with the girl because he doesn't respect her mentor. In the meantime, George becomes a mentor. George gets the protégé to read a text book on risk management because he needs someone to explain the topic to him for a New York Yankees job.

Aside from this fictional Seinfeld episode, having a mentor is a very, very, very, very, very good idea—and that's a lot of verys.

Later on, you'll read about my general disdain for ladder climbing. I mention that because this may seem like contradictory advice. It is my book, however, and I will take offense if you insist on pointing out flaws in my writing.

Telling you to find a mentor to guide you on your career journey is not a green light to blindly try to shimmy up the corporate ladder. I'm simply trying to impart that a mentor can help tremendously if you do want a different job, even if it's a lateral move. A mentor can also help you feel happier in the job you have.

Scary as it may be, in my own flawed way, I'm trying to mentor you with this book. A better arrangement, however, would be to find a mentor at your company, so you can get coaching and support from someone who actually knows what you do for a living.

I'm not going to sugarcoat this. Finding a worthy mentor could be like finding an icy cold beverage in hell, but you can do it.

There are two benefits of having a mentor:

1. A mentor will guide your rudderless life toward greater happiness at work. Be prepared though. Following through with your mentor's suggestions might entail effort and, for that, I'm sorry.

2. If you want to kick it up a notch, find a mentor with influence. People around the office will indubitably notice immediately and this will yield all kinds of street cred.

In closing, when you find someone who generously gives you a helping hand with your career, don't be an ungrateful bastard. Thank the person. A nice gesture would be to buy your mentor a nice gift, like some malt liquor or beef jerky.

Stellar Gem #16: Flee Toxic People

This is my last TV reference, unless I change my mind and decide to include another one.

Do you remember the Saturday Night Live Debbie Downer skit?

If you're scratching your head and it's not lice-related, it's okay. The theme song sums Debbie up pretty well. Here's a snippet: ". . . she's always there to tell you about a new disease, a car accident or killer bees . . ."

You probably know someone at work like Debbie—a dark cloud always doing his or her best to block out the sun. That type of person is toxic.

Question: When faced with a toxic substance, what is the appropriate course of action?

a. Lick it.

b. Pour it down your pants.

c. Rub it behind your ear in the hope of attracting a mate.

d. Stay as far away from it as possible.

Ding, ding, ding. The correct answer is "d."

At work, you hopefully aren't exposed to actual toxic waste. You do, however, need to steer clear of toxic people like Debbie because their bleak outlook will suck you deep into their black hole of negativity. If you allow that to happen, here's just a sampling of what's in store for you:

- You'll become despondent.

- You'll cease to enjoy ice cream, puppies, and rainbows.

- You'll obsessively listen to tragic country music ballads.

In short, the modestly happy life you've built will be over.

Wait. What?

My mind-reading abilities are telling me you're thinking: "Hey genius, that's great, but if I work with the person, how do you propose I avoid him?"

Well, that feels harsh and abusive, but I'll attempt to answer your question nonetheless.

To avoid toxic co-workers, you have two options:

1. **Covert avoidance.** Think Jason Bourne here. No, scratch that. No need to go off the grid. Instead, simply study the movements of your Debbie Downer and then use that knowledge to avoid her.

2. **Overt avoidance.** Alternatively, if you're the gutsy sort, you could flat out tell "Debbie" she's toxic. More specifically, you could say something like: "Hey Debbie, you're toxic sludge and I want nothing to do with you. I learned all about you in a fantastic, reasonably priced book." Then be prepared to get punched in the throat.

Now take a break and go enjoy some Saturday Night Live.

Stellar Gem #17: Fake It 'Til You Make It

Have you ever heard this expression? I first heard it from my social worker wife. It has a lot of practical application for all of us trying to survive work.

In therapy, I think "Fake it 'til you make it" means that you should act like the person you want to become and, eventually, you'll turn into that desirable person you've been impersonating.

Whoa. That's deep.

I'm no Sigmund Freud, but it sounds plausible.

Let's say you arrive at work and it's the last place on God's green earth you want to be. I know, hard to fathom.

Every time you feel this way, you've reached a fork in the road and you have a choice to make. You can choose to be cantankerous, making everyone around you miserable, or you can force yourself to be positive and keep the old chin up until you begin to feel better.

Correct. You should do the latter.

"Screw that!" you say?

I understand your hostility. I also know that you have valid reasons to be in a pissy mood. You hate your job and you want the world to know.

Here's the rub though. Tons of people are in the same boat. We'll call that boat the USS Misery and there are so many people onboard, it's a miracle it's still afloat.

Our colleagues don't want to hear us bitch and moan. Besides, where does stewing in your own juices get you? Nowhere, and it will ruin your health.

Give it a try. It may take an hour or more, but maybe you can power through the bad mood.

Stellar Gem #18: Spruce Up That Carpeted Jail Cell

Get out your pencil. We're going to do a little math.

Subtract the number of hours in a day you spend asleep. Got it?

Good. Now subtract the time you spend working.

Finally, look at what's left and stick your head in the oven.

No, I'm kidding. Please don't do that.

You have to admit though, it's a serious downer when you consider that we spend substantially more time at work than we do with our friends and family. Think about this as you're sitting in a cubicle (a.k.a. your carpeted jail cell) and you may feel clinically depressed.

If you spend time trapped in a cubicle, wouldn't it make sense to try and make that space as homey as possible?

You'd think so, right? Yet, over the years, time and again, I've noticed some people expend zero effort trying to spruce up their carpeted jail cells. I'm not only talking about new hires either. I've seen people at a company for many years who don't have a single photo or personal effect. Strange.

What about you? The next time you sit down at your desk, look around. What do you see? If the answer is nothing, maybe that's partly to blame for your perpetual grim mood.

Believe me, I get it if you have an indifferent attitude. However, to one degree or another, our work environment plays a role in how we feel. When you look at it that way, why not make your surroundings a bit more cheerful?

The good news is that if you're cubicle is currently as cheery as the city morgue, sprucing it up can be cheap and easy. Here are four options:

1. **Photos.** Display a picture of your family. If your family is grotesque, display a picture of a Golden Retriever or the attractive family that came with the frame.

2. **Cartoons (or other funny stuff).** You should always have something funny at your desk because life is absurd and you have to find the humor in it. Personally, I love Far Side® cartoons. Also, if it stops making you laugh, swap it out for something else. I have a plaque that says: "Get to work. You're not being paid to believe in the power of your dreams." In the background is a serious picture, totally mocking those dumb "inspirational" posters about teamwork, leadership, etc.

3. **Plants.** I see a lot of women with plants at their desks, but not guys for some reason. Plants add color, clean the air, and make being at work more pleasant. Even if you're as brown-thumbed as I am, you can find plants that are nearly impossible to kill.

4. **Accessories.** No, I'm not talking about your belt. Coffee mug, maybe a nice clock, you know, that sort of thing.

Hope this helps.

Stellar Gem #19: Steer Clear of Vending Machines

If sitting near vending machines excites you, that's truly sad. While I'm filled with pity for you, I also understand how you might be seduced by their allure. After all, vending machines offer refreshment and who doesn't like to feel refreshed?

But you need to steer clear of vending machines because they are filled with "food" that will make you unhealthy and they're a rip off.

If that weren't bad enough, vending machines pose a bigger problem. It's a problem you've probably never thought of and it affects anyone forced to sit near a vending machine.

At this point you are understandably confused, so allow me to clear things up.

Sitting close to a vending machine sucks because vending machines are a gathering place for people who engage in inane chatter.

These people love the sound of their own voice. They blather on and on, loudly and persistently. Those unlucky enough to be within earshot are consequently forced to listen to all kinds of nonsense.

I've noticed two varieties of blabber-mouths whose chatter makes it hard to concentrate:

1. **The Deliberator.** "Hey Gary, do you think I should get a Milky Way or the Snickers bar? I could really go for a Snickers, but I don't know if I'm in the mood for nuts right now. But then again, nuts are an awesome source of protein and they say having a little protein in the afternoon is the way to go. It's hard because they're both delicious. Oh, the heck with it . . . I'm just going to get the Snickers. I can always come back for a Milky Way later. There seem to be a lot of them left so I don't have to worry about them running out."

2. **The Justifier.** "Oh, hey. I didn't see you standing there. Yeah, I'm just getting myself some powdered donuts and a gargantuan cola to wash them down. I wasn't going to, but I've been good this week."

The icing on the highly processed, two-month-old snack cake, however, is when these gadflies saunter up to your desk. They will interrupt you because a dollar bill isn't working in the machine and they'll petition you to help.

You should reply: "Oh yes, please. I was working on something extremely important and time sensitive. But sure, let me take your filthy crumpled paper currency and provide you with crisp new bill. I wouldn't want you to miss snack time."

Steer clear of those vending machines! Steer clear, I tell you!

Stellar Gem #20: Remember, You're the Real Rock Star

My last tip for this section of the book is to always remember that you're the real rock star.

That's because you, my friend, make this country great. That's right, you. Not some stoned drummer. Not some illiterate athlete. Not some perfect looking Hollywood actor. Not some ruthless corporate CEO.

If you don't believe me, it's only because we live in a royally screwed up culture and you've been brainwashed to think a person's worth is directly tied to his or her wealth. Those inclined to disagree with me need only look at a lot of the people who earn the highest incomes.

Many of the wealthiest among us have done nothing to cure disease or help the poor. They are not taking care of the elderly. They are not ending hunger. Many simply won the womb lottery.

As far as the celebs, don't get me wrong. I love movies, TV, music, and sports. I also genuinely admire artistic and athletic talent, but give me a break. It's nothing short of obscene how much some of those people get paid.

And don't even get me started on corporate executives. Have you ever wondered how CEOs justify earning more in a year than a rank-and-file person earns in a lifetime? The answer is simple. It can't be justified. Their compensation is in the stratosphere, even when their companies do poorly. It's ridiculous.

If you're incensed about the chasm between the 1% and ordinary Americans, you should be. I don't know how to change all this. Just remember that you are the real rock star.

Why? Because your hard work matters—a lot.

I'm not blowing smoke either. It's the God's honest truth.

I don't see an end to our culture putting the wrong people on pedestals. My only advice is to keep plugging away, doing your thing.

Also, even though you are a rock star, don't get any ideas about running amok in the office playing air guitar. No one wants to see that.

WAYS TO SUCCEED

You'll notice that I did not entitle this section "Ways to Advance Your Career." As you're about to learn, I'm not a big proponent of blind ambition. Also, I frankly don't care if you get a promotion. Sorry to be blunt, but honesty is the best policy.

This next set of gems isn't a road map to the corner office. However, if you abide by these rules, you'll get a glowing year-end appraisal and a massive raise, or maybe 1%.

Stellar Gem #21: Settle Down Hot Shot

For the life of me, I can't figure out why there's so much ambition in corporate America. I mean, really. Taking classes after working all day, volunteering for extra projects, staying late and schmoozing with anyone who has the power to promote you. It's like some sort of competition to see who can withstand the most aggravation and stress.

I'd like to suggest we all take a deep breath and think about what we're doing.

Don't get me wrong. I love money. Truth be told, I might marry a pile of hundreds if I could, but good God. How low are we willing to stoop to acquire more money?

I won't go so far as to say that promotions are inherently bad. I mean, if the notion of chasing a fancier job title at work makes you as giddy as a school girl, go for it. I wish you good luck.

However, if the only seduction of a promotion is more money, don't take the bait (unless you're so financially down on your luck that you're contemplating drug dealing and pyramid schemes to make ends meet.) Also, don't jump at a promotion for the prestige because, frankly, no one is impressed.

Yes, there will be times when the grass will look greener elsewhere and maybe it is.

On the other hand, you have to be prepared for the possibility that the grass will be dead and full of dog poo.

I realize this may make me sound like a raging pessimist. I'm not though. I'm only 21% pessimist and 79% straight shooter.

It comes down to this: I can't bear to watch you make bonehead career move you'll regret. I've met too many nice people like you who say yes to a promotion only to be made miserable—or more miserable (yes, it's possible) by some new, "better" job.

If all that doesn't dampen your corporate ladder climbing ambitions, remember that on your deathbed, you won't lament that you didn't spend more time at the office.

Maybe instead of burning the midnight oil and devoting your free time absorbed in books about synergy and Six Sigma, spend that precious time with loved ones.

Stellar Gem #22: Make Yourself Comfortable

Before I pour even more priceless knowledge into that noggin of yours, indulge me. Please tell me know how you'd finish each of these sentences:

1. When I watch my favorite television program, I like to:

    a) Sink into my favorite Barcalounger and relax.

    b) Recline in a tub filled with broken glass, rusty nails, and scorpions.

2. When I'm weary at the end of the day, I typically:

    a) Climb into my soft, cozy bed and rest my weary head on a fluffy down pillow.

    b) Force myself to stay awake by eating coffee grounds and sticking ice cubes down my pants.

If you answered "b" in either scenario, quickly go make an appointment with your neighborhood mental health professional.

For those who answered "a" to these questions, congratulations! You're not a nut job. You're rational. You're normal. You, understandably, wish to be comfortable.

I'm afraid, however, that this simple notion is lost on many corporate people. At work, choosing what's comfortable and familiar is akin to some sort of sickness that requires immediate medical attention.

God forbid it ever suffice for an employee to simply be a reliable and a consistent contributor to the success of an organization. Oh no, that would never do. We all need to get out of our "comfort zone" and "stretch ourselves."

Well, if you propagate this sort of baloney, please stop it. There's absolutely nothing wrong with being comfortable. Plus, at work, it's not usually even an issue of comfortable or uncomfortable. It's about personal preference.

For example, introverted employees avoid public speaking because they don't like speaking in public. Creative people don't prepare taxes because they'd rather wrestle a grizzly bear.

If you want to force yourself to do things you hate and fear, have at it. Go stretch the heck out of yourself, but don't impose that ridiculous rule on the rest of us.

For those in my corner, if someone at work starts blathering on about stretching yourself, tell them to bugger off, or stand up for yourself in some other way. And you might also want to throw in that if you wanted to stretch yourself, you'd go sign up for a yoga class.

Will there by times that you need to step up and do things at work that make you uncomfortable? Yes, of course, and that's fine.

When that happens, do what needs to be done and get it over with. Don't, however, be goaded into saying yes to something that makes you uncomfortable because some tool says you'll come out of it a better, happier human being.

Stellar Gem #23: Be Pseudo Indispensable

If you're a non-retired adult, you probably like to feel needed at work. That's understandable.

It feels good to be needed. Plus, when you're useful, you improve your chances of not getting fired. That, in turn, gives you a steady stream of moolah that you can use to pay your bills and buy a lot of useless crap you don't need.

You gotta know where to draw the line though. You mustn't allow yourself to become indispensable.

No, that's not a typo.

It's understandable if you're under the impression that being indispensable is something to which you should aspire. It's a common misconception.

What could be wrong with mastering a skill or two?

A lot. Trust me.

One terrible scenario involves you being the ONLY employee who has mastery of a skill.

See where this is going?

Yea, every time task X needs doing (think weekly if not daily), guess what? You get to do it. Lucky duck!

Then one day you want to put in for the day off so you can go to a business person's special or the beach, but nope. Not happening. You have to complete task X, and no one else knows how to do it.

That'll teach you to apply yourself and nobly step up to learn a sought-after skill.

Try and make it clear you're not up to it. Self-sabotage could work too. Botch your first attempt and the boss will have no choice but to move on and tap the next sucker, er, I mean, rising star.

Stellar Gem #24: Grin and Bear It

This one is insanely hard.

As you know, the amount of nonsense workers contend with in corporate America is staggering. What makes it worse is when management is close-minded and refuses to listen to reason or dissenting viewpoints.

For sure, senior management and human resources will say they treasure your feedback, and that they prize honesty and open dialogue. Yea. Not true.

An employee could be spot on with an assessment of a situation. The feedback could be delivered intelligently and articulately. The feedback could illustrate how a process or technology adoption makes no sense, maybe to the point where it's creating harm.

Honesty, no one wants to hear it.

Despite many messages to the contrary, many companies do not value input from the peons. They'd much prefer low level workers not rock the boat. Fall in line. Smile. Keep critical comments to yourself.

I think it goes back to ego and lack of humility. I don't know how else to explain it. I feel like it's akin to your doctor sending you an email saying you should stop exercising, take up smoking, and eat more junk food. After the shock wore off, even though you didn't go to medical school, you reply and lay out why you think those are terrible ideas.

She insists. You relent. Three months later at a follow-up appointment:

You: I feel like the cigarettes and potato chips you recommended aren't making me healthier.

Doctor: Well, I'm much smarter than you.

Patient: Okay, but I've read dozens of articles saying those things are incredibly unhealthy.

Doctor: I see. Hmm, look at the time. Here's what I want you to do. Let's ramp up the smoking and I want to switch from the regular potato chips to barbeque.

As you try to process and formulate a response, she's off to spread her bad advice to the next patient.

This phenomenon in corporate America is astonishing. It defies logic. It truly makes you feel like you're living inside a Dilbert cartoon.

"Grin and bear it" is very sucky advice, so I don't want to end with that. Maybe slightly better: Grin and bear it, at least until you can find a new place to work, one where your views are respected.

Stellar Gem #25: Watch Out for Shrapnel

I'm far too cowardly to serve in the military, but I'm extremely grateful to all the brave souls who have served.

While it's true I have zero soldiering experience, I have spent many years in the cubicle trenches and I'm here to tell you—it's a war zone.

How does one survive? Rule #1: Keep your head down. When all hell breaks loose (again), things may start to explode. Forget to keep your head down and you're going to get hit with the shrapnel, and I've seen enough war movies to know that you don't want to get hit by shrapnel.

Where are the grenades? Everywhere! A grenade explodes every time a:

• Project goes horribly wrong.

• Staff meeting goes horribly wrong.

• Sales presentation goes horribly wrong.

• Company picnic goes horribly wrong.

• Relationship goes horribly wrong.

You get the idea.

The good news is, just like you have some time to take cover once a hand grenade pin is pulled, corporate grenades usually provide a small window of time to escape. What I mean is you can frequently see a danger growing. That's when it's time to get out of sight and lay low until the smoke clears.

"Isn't hiding cowardly?" you ask. Yes. What's your point? This isn't some Allies versus the Nazis battle with human life and freedom hanging in the balance. It's just a lot of corporate idiocy.

My preferred hiding spot is a bathroom stall, but hide wherever you like. Behind a potted plant could also work nicely.

Also, it's not enough to hide. You must also be quiet as a ninja, lest you be discovered and pulled into the fray.

I will admit, it isn't always easy to run and hide. For example, you might be in a meeting sitting a long way from the door. Even if you made a break for it, your boss might track you down with Bloodhounds.

Worst of all, you could be asked to chime in. When this happens, remain mute and offer a blank stare. If that doesn't work, say something neutral and benign like: "Hmm, let me give that some thought."

You should also maintain a grave look on your face. This will communicate to others that you take the whole stupid matter very seriously. You'll want to do this even though you have no idea what got everyone so flustered.

Stellar Gem #26: Beware the Corporate Wedgie

It's impossible not to have pet peeves at work. The older I get, the more of them I have. At last count, I have 34,658.

Soon, like next week, I'll be in a perpetual state of irritation. In a few years, my peeves will finally push me over the edge and I'll spend the rest of my days rocking back in forth in a mental ward singing the theme song from The Love Boat. Maybe you'll be a good friend and visit me. We could rock and sing together.

Right now, however, I want to discuss a huge pet peeve, maybe the biggest. I call it the corporate wedgie, a name I came up with a few minutes ago.

First, let's review the traditional wedgie. While I've never personally administered or received a traditional wedgie, I know the basics. It happens when some half-wit bully decides to yank some poor nerd's underwear straight up, inflicting ample pain and humiliation. The bully gets a hearty laugh out of this.

In the socially challenging world of high school, the fact that a wedgie is a thing comes as no surprise. Unfortunate for sure, but it seems there always has been, and always will be, big stupid kids who get off on preying on smaller, weaker kids.

Thank God it ends in high school. Oh wait. The hell it does.

You only think the wedgie nonsense is over when you graduate from high school. College provides a respite, then a different kind of wedgie emerges in adulthood—the corporate wedgie.

When there's a bully at work, no need to worry about your underwear. It's in no danger of getting stuck in your butt crack. You have bigger problems.

High school lasts four years. Your career will last 40 years or more.

Here's what to look out for:

- **A corporate bully is vicious.** You think you have a good relationship with someone and then something goes wrong. Then that person eviscerates you in front of others to save their own skin.

- **A corporate bully can't be trusted.** He or she will be nice to your face and talk badly about you as soon as you're out of the room.

- **A corporate bully is insecure.** You want to feel sympathy for the bully, although knowing the person is insecure doesn't help much. You want to see the good in the person. Then the bully perpetrates another evil act.

Don't despair. All bullies, regardless of age, have one thing in common—they count on the victims not standing up for themselves.

Don't put up with it.

Stellar Gem #27: Step It Up Slacker

Dads can teach you a lot, like how to ride a bike, throw a ball, drink beer, belch, and so on. One thing my father drilled into me was to be a self-starter.

I undoubtedly rolled my eyes as a kid upon hearing this pragmatic advice. These many years later, his paternal wisdom has stuck with me, especially in the context of work. I mean really, what employer doesn't love a self-starter?

A lot of people will tell you that brilliant people make the best employees. Not necessarily.

Don't get me wrong. Brainy is great. However, intellect isn't always the best predictor of career success.

Sure, some brilliant people make fantastic employees. On the other hand, some of the smartest people I've ever worked with have also been the laziest.

For all of us who didn't graduate from an Ivy League college with a perfect 4.0 grade point average, rejoice! We can still be successful, provided we take some initiative.

For those of you who recently started a new job, being a self-starter might be tough. You might still be learning the ropes and it might sometimes be tough to even recognize what work needs to be done.

It's okay. If you're in this boat, you can still impress that boss of yours, and anyone else you're looking to win favor with.

How exactly?

You can do this by asking a lot questions. You can't ask too many, so set a lofty goal. Three hundred questions a day should do it.

Asking questions isn't hard, and it demonstrates that you're eager and want to be a self-starter.

Dad, thanks for imparting this useful gem. By some miracle, it seeped into my pea brain and stayed there.

Someday I hope my son will look back and thank me for at least one thing I taught him. I'd prefer that thing not be belching, but if it is, so be it.

Now, go figure out what needs attention, roll up those shirt sleeves, and get to work.

Stellar Gem #28: Communicate Like a Pro

Fact: People suck at communicating.* This causes all sorts of unnecessary problems and general unpleasantness, both at work and in the world at large.

Issues created by poor communication run the gamut from inconsequential to severe.

Getting the wrong pizza topping might be followed by some sadness, mild and temporary, assuming you're normal. If it sends you into a deep depression, you have bigger issues.

On the serious side, bad communication leads to real problems, like unhappy customers, financial loss, and damaged or ruined relationships with colleagues.

If you can move into the small minority who have first-rate communication skills, you'll run into less frustration and enjoy more success. Sound good?

Great, now just stick to my top 3 rules and you'll be golden.

1. **Try not to ramble.** Whether you're writing or speaking at work, rambling is never good. It leads to mistakes and co-workers will then will have no choice but to burn you in effigy. Get to the point and don't waste people's time.

   Some think that brevity and laziness are synonymous. Au contraire. Being able to quickly and effectively convey a message is a tremendous skill.

2. **Be clear.** Your writing or speech should never cause confusion. If a cloud of fog forms around the audience's heads, you've failed miserably.

   If you doubt clarity is crucial, consider The Centers for Disease Control and Prevention (CDC). The CDC was a revered organization, and then the COVID epidemic hit.

   Brilliant scientific minds? For sure. Effective communicators? Hardly.

Inconsistent and confusing guidance caused tremendous harm to the CDC's reputation and greatly eroded people's confidence in the organization. Yep, they learned the hard way.

3. **Keep it simple.** Plain is always better than fancy. Maybe you know some great SAT words. That's swell. No one wants to see or hear them. Save that vocabulary for your novel. In business, even if the material you need to present is complex, the best thing you can do for your audience is to dumb it down.

---

*Few among us will admit to sucking at communicating. On the contrary, many will swear on a stack of bibles that they are stellar at it. Kinda like how everyone thinks they are hilarious and awesome at driving.

Stellar Gem #29: Add Random Letters After Your Name

You should never feel like you have to impress anyone.

Ha, that's absurd! You likely try to impress all kind of people. I don't precisely know who in your case. Your boss, a crush, maybe the mailman. It really doesn't matter.

There are different ways you can impress someone. One way is to run into a burning building to save a baby or a litter of kittens. Then you could start speaking flawless French and really wow them.

Or you could add some letters after your name. You know, a credential or multiple credentials.

If you don't see where I'm going with this, imagine Joe Smith. Joe's a regular dude until he gets his PhD in 14th century Bulgarian lute playing. Then the rest of us have to call him a doctor even though he can't even prescribe an aspirin.

PhD is one example. There are, however, all kinds of professional designations out there. No matter what line of work you're in, there's likely some string of letters that would boost your professional credibility like RN, CPA, LCSW, and CFP, so on and so forth.

Tragically, earning the right to put a legitimate designation after your name can entail hard work. You'll have to study and pass one or more exams. Then after you acquire what you seek, you may be forced to regularly take continuing education to maintain the designation. I'm exhausted just thinking about it.

Luckily, there's no need to bother yourself with all that. That's because there are so many kooky designations in this world, most people don't have a clue what the letters mean, and their certainly not going to check to see if you actually have earned said credential.

See where I'm going with this?

What I'm suggesting is you add some random letters after your name. This in turn will help you garner respect and advance your career.

Hey, don't look so surprised. I'm simply proposing the path of least resistance. If anything, you should be commending me for the brilliant efficiency of my idea.

Anyway, when selecting your letters, don't invest a lot of time in the task. You have better things to do with your time, like polishing your shoes or attending to your ant farm.

My only advice is not to pick something that sounds too phony baloney. And don't use a string of letters that spells something dirty, although it would be fun to see those on your business card.

Once you've settled on your new letters, congratulations! Display them all on correspondence for all the world to see. I also recommend getting a name plate for your desk engraved with your new fake designation. Then sit back and watch your street cred grow.

Stellar Gem #30: Sport Some Specs

Wearing glasses makes you look smarter, no matter how much of a dolt you are. I even read this on the internet once, which means it has to be true.

Now, you'll need to do one of three things:

- If you already wear glasses, congratulations on your imperfect vision. Please skip ahead to the next gem.

- If you wear contacts, stop being so vain. Who are you, Dorian Gray? Lose the contacts and get yourself a nice pair of spectacles.

- If you have perfect vision and don't need glasses, wear them anyway.*

Give it a try and you'll be amazed. Mosey around the office in a pair of fashionable frames, people will be in awe of your brilliance.

When purchasing your new glasses, stay away from thin lenses. There's a direct correlation between lens thickness and perceived IQ. The thicker the lens the smarter people will think you are.

Since I'm not a total control freak, please feel free to buy whatever frames that catch your eye. I think we can all agree that's pretty big of me.

Also, while wearing your glasses, it's important to never smile. That's because a blank, emotionless countenance will make you look even more studious and impressive. Given you'll be at work, not smiling should be a piece of cake.

Next, remember to take your glasses off from time to time, preferably in a dramatic fashion. For added effect, furrow your brow and put the end of one of the ear pieces in your mouth. These tactics are especially effective in meetings. You'll look like a U.S. Senator holding a hearing.

Finally, don't look at purchasing a pair of glasses as a financial expense. Look at it as more of an investment in your career, a small toll to pay to be put on a pedestal.

*I've only known one person who wore glasses and didn't need them. I don't remember the chap's name, but he and I washed dishes together back in 1986. This dude wasn't trying to look smart though. It was more of a fashion statement and I suppose that's okay too. When I wasn't washing dishes with Mr. Fashion, I was washing dishes with a good-natured, somewhat insane Russian man. Good times.

Stellar Gem #31: Wait Here Personal Problems

Ah, problems. What would life be without them?

I'm sure you've had your share. Maybe a significant other broke your heart. Maybe your washing machine died. Maybe your cat is upset with you because you brought home the wrong brand of treats. Let's not get hung up on details.

Suffice to say, problems are unavoidable and it's a bummer when bad things befalls nice people like you and me.

Nevertheless, unless you're facing something truly dire, you need to suck it up and check these distractions at the door before you head into work.

Don't think you can? Well, that's only because you're weak and undisciplined and, quite frankly, you disgust me.

No, I'm just kidding. You're great.

Now, where was I?

Oh yes. To adequately motivate you, I hereby falsely promise that adhering to this guidance will make you 78% happier and more successful.

Here are some additional instructions to follow:

1. **Accept the fact that no one wants to listen to you bitch and moan.** Everyone has their sack of rocks to carry in life. While complaining may be cathartic to you, it might be immensely irritating to other people.

2. **Throw yourself into whatever work lies in front of you.** Stop harping on your problems. They're a distraction. Instead, put your nose to the grindstone, whatever the hell a grindstone is.

By concentrating on your work, you'll temporarily forget about your problems. You'll feel less distress and the quality of your work will improve.

People at work will also forget about your past transgressions and start to think you might even be a good egg instead of a no-good, whiny son of a bitch. Then, before you know it, they'll be offering you some great new job, like Head Lackey or Vice President of the Office Supply Closets.

Besides, your personal problems will be patiently waiting for you after work ends. Personal problems are very loyal that way.

Stellar Gem #32: Stop Being a Jackass (or an Elephant)

Are you a Democrat or a Republican? Maybe you fancy the Green Party.

That's great, but talking politics can get you into trouble.

Hey, I'm not saying a love of politics is bad. In fact, there's too much apathy in this country, so I think your interest in politics is admirable and I'll be right there with you on election day doing my part to support our tremendously dysfunctional government.

Now that I've clarified, if you're talking about controversial political topics at work, you might want to give it a rest.

If you're ranting about politics, it's only a matter of time before your views rub someone the wrong way. Granted, it may not matter much if you upset your peers, but pissing off management is another matter.

Political discourse in our country has never been worse. Citizens are constantly gravitating to one extreme or another. So, consider biting your tongue if you're tempted to spout off about one of your extreme viewpoints.

If you're ultra conservative, for example, don't launch into a two-hour rant about how the government is trying to take away your guns. Or, on the other side of things, if you're a bleeding-heart liberal, don't lecture people on your extreme policy ideas, like extending Social Security and Medicare benefits to elderly dogs and cats.

Another thing. Even if your boss is fine with your political views, he or she might be perturbed if you're debates are taking you away from your work.

"Hey, I'm passionate about politics. Leave me alone."

Okay, okay.

I've mostly said my peace. I'll end with a simple suggestion.

Rather than airing your political views at work, save it for later. A compromise of sorts. Once you punch out for the day, have at it. Talk politics till your heart's content.

Possibilities abound for political discourse. Go online and type feverishly until the wee hours of the morning. Or go down to the local donut shop. Donuts and coffee go great with political discussion.

Stellar Gem #33: Make Your Math Teacher Proud

Pop quiz: If I order a pizza and give you the entire pizza, what percentage of the pizza have I given you?

The correct answer: 100%.

Okay, let's try another one. A colleague has just given everything he had creating a boring spreadsheet. How much effort has he expended?

(A) 100%

(B) 110%

(C) 120%

(D) 1,000,000%

Hint: This is not a trick question.

Yes, the answer is still 100%.

If you answered anything other than 100%, your math teacher's life's work was in vain. Please go write him or her an apology letter.

Where did this math abuse originate? I blame sports broadcasters and athletes. They're constantly crediting athletes with giving 110%.

I've come up with an official sounding name for this dumb phenomenon. Not that you care, but I've come up with the name Excessive Percentage Allocation to describe instances when people make these mathematically impossible claims. Yes, naming it was pointless, but so are many of the things I do.

At work, usage of Excessive Percentage Allocation is worse than in the sports world.

I say that because, at least with sports, you can change the station.

If you're routinely guilty of this math violation, please stop.

I hope this written admonishment will suffice. If you persist, I will find out. When I do, I'll be left with no other choice than to enroll you in a remedial math class.

Stellar Gem #34: Scribble on Your Whiteboard

Regardless of how inept you are, you need to convince others that you're Mr. or Ms. Highly Competent. You also want them to think that you're swamped with vital tasks that will reshape the future of the organization.

You will accomplish this using your whiteboard.

I can only assume you have a whiteboard if you're a cubicle dweller. Not having one would be akin to a mechanic not having a wrench.

To get optimal benefit from your whiteboard:

1. Divide your board into two halves, left and right.

2. On the left, write down something that will impress the casual walker by. For example, you might want to write "1p.m. – Lunch with *<insert CEO name>*." Or scribble a phrase that incorporates some idiotic corporate vocabulary, like "Maximize synergies" or "Future state parity." For added effect, add a question mark at the end, as if you're grappling with something hefty that could easily take several months to resolve.

3. The right-hand side of your board will be reserved for mathematical equations. Luckily, unless you work in an engineering firm, it can be anything. That's because we're basically a nation of math illiterates. No one will be able recognize that your equation is completely made up. For example, you could jot this down "$65 + \pi = 87.51 \geq 52$." This will help cement your rep as the office genius.

4. If space allows, I strongly recommend adding a chart with green arrows shooting upward to show you're hard at work making the organization more profitable. To accomplish this, make sure the y axis (yes, that's the one that goes up and down) shows a dollar sign. Then, along the x axis (yes, that's the one that goes from left to right), write "Revenue" or "Profit."

5. Last, but not least, whatever you do, don't write neatly because geniuses never have good handwriting. Anyone who's ever seen a doctor's signature on a prescription knows this to be true.

All of this will send a strong message to any passersby that you're simply too busy being brilliant to be interrupted.

Lastly, since you're brilliant, don't be a dummy and write on your board with a permanent marker. The marker says "permanent" right on the side of it for God's sake.

Stellar Gem #35: Dress Shabbily

At one time or another, someone has probably told you to dress for success. This well-intentioned person is mistaken.

The person was suggesting that, if you regularly look sharp and polished, you'll have the world by the cojones. Well, that's absurd.

"Dress for success" is complete rubbish. If you waltz around the office looking like a hundred million bucks, people will assume you're some rich jerk. And they'll hate you for the financial good fortune they believe you've found.

I have the opposite philosophy. I'm convinced you should think differently about it, or "examine it under a different lens," if you want to sound like a corporate jackass.

If you'd like your wardrobe to help you in your career, that's superficial, but I guess I can't stop you. All I can do is make suggestions.

My advice: When you open your closet door or dresser drawer, don't pull out duds that make you look like hedge fund manager or a funeral home director. Instead, grab the ugliest, most tattered rags you own and put them on. In short, dress as shabbily as possible.

Ugh, your skepticism is exhausting. Luckily, I'm a great guy with a lot of patience, so I'll continue to try and persuade you.

Think of it this way. Show up at the office looking like a hobo and people will pity you.

Now, many people will tell you being the object of others pity is a bad thing. No, no, no! Having people pity you is highly desirable because it'll result in everyone being nicer to you.

It will be as if every day is your birthday, minus the cake and ironic greeting cards. And the icing on your nonexistent birthday cake—colleagues will also want to help you financially since you look down on your luck.

Picture this: You waltz in wearing dirty, tattered, ill-fitting clothing and your kindly colleagues gather to take up a collection for you. Who knows how much they'll raise? Someone might even sponsor a "fun run" or a beef & beer fundraiser.

To top it off, a mean their boss's icy heart might start to melt. He or she might be moved by your tragic appearance. Then a hefty raise or bonus will surely be in the offing.

If you already have a ratty wardrobe, nice job! You're good to go.

If any of your clothing says Armani or Gucci, lock those garments away in your closet. Then clear your calendar because this weekend you'll be heading over to your local thrift store for some "new" threads. Make sure you bring at least $6. That should be enough to finance the wardrobe I have in mind for you.

Stellar Gem #36: Quit Staring at Your Shoes

Time for a pop quiz. Let's say you're walking down the hallway and you pass a colleague. Please identify the *inappropriate* response from the options listed below.

(A) Say hello.

(B) Smile.

(C) Pay the person a compliment.

(D) Say nothing and stare intently at your shoes.

If you answered D, you need to read this.

It's baffling why someone you're acquainted with, someone who's not your enemy, would completely ignore you, sometimes on a daily basis. Not your ticket to the c-suite or wherever you want to work next.

Hey, you don't want to speak, that's fine. Believe me, I get it. Silence is refreshing, but passing someone without acknowledging their existence is seriously awkward. If using your vocal cords to utter "hello" is too much of a strain, how about a head nod? Surely you can manage that.

I've walked past people I've known for years who repeatedly pull this move. It's rude and bizarre. Who wouldn't want to say hello to me? I'm so lovable.

I've never seen anyone called out on this antisocial behavior. If I did, I wonder what sort of lame excuses I'd hear from the shoe gazer. What rationale would someone possibly give to explain why they refuse to make eye contact and remain mute?

Here are some of the excuses I imagine I'd hear along with my spot-on rebuttals:

Excuse	Rebuttal
I'm shy.	I am too, but I don't stare at my shoes.
I'm tired.	I am too, but I don't stare at my shoes.
I'm in a bad mood.	I am too, but I don't stare at my shoes.
"My shoes cost more than your car so I like to admire them.	You're a jackass.

Seriously, if you look down when you pass someone in the corridor, your co-workers are most definitely forming negative impressions about you. They'll probably think you're a sociopath.

Make a little eye contact, muster a smile, and say hi. It's not that hard.

By the way, if you want to say more, wonderful, but please don't ask me how I'm doing. I've always hated when people mindlessly blurt this out as a substitute for saying hi. Unless you actually do care and wish to listen to my woes, don't ask. If you do care to hear about my problems, clear your calendar. I'll need at least 3 or 4 hours to get everything off my chest.

Stellar Gem #37: Change Your Name to Dr. Bullshit

You seem like a stand-up person. I also bet you've been walking around believing that your honesty, integrity, and hard work are enough.

It's a common misconception.

That misconception is why, tomorrow morning, I want you to march down to city hall and officially change your name to Dr. Bullshit. Please remember to bring a photo ID.

Once you've legally changed your name, it's time to start backing up your new name by spewing rubbish at work like there's no tomorrow. It's a guaranteed way to advance your career.

The bullshit is so deep in corporate America employee should be wearing fishing waders. By my estimation, success is about 0.5% knowing what you're talking about and 99.5% sounding like you know what you're talking about.

If you're like me, what I'm suggesting does not come naturally, but that's okay.

People like us just need to remember to:

- **Be confident.** No need to worry about how outlandish your statements at work might seem. You can say whatever absurd, untrue thing you can think of as long as you say it with conviction.

- **Keep yammering.** When you're in the zone, giving some made-up explanation about why something went wrong, keep on talking. Your unrelenting verbal assault on your colleagues will assure no one gets a word in edgewise. This will reduce the chances of anyone cutting in to dispute your factually-challenged statements.

- **Stand your ground.** If someone does challenge your absurd assertions, don't be fazed or lose your composure. Just keep applying more and more bullshit until you've won her over or exhausted him into submission.

- **Smile.** Being disarming is a characteristic you'll find in all good bullshitters and there's nothing more disarming than a bright smile. That's why, unless you're chewing a baloney sandwich, you should always be flashing your pearly whites.

In the world of movies, no one is better at this than Ferris Bueller. So go watch Ferris Bueller's Day Off again for some inspiration.

Start doling it out and be running your company in no time.

Stellar Gem #38: Show Up

Woody Allen is best known for his funny movies, but he also had some pretty astute things to say over the years. For example, he once said: "Eighty percent of success is showing up."

Definitely words to live by.

Do you lack even a rudimentary understanding of how to do your job? No sweat. Simply show up for work at the appointed time, or close to it, and your success is all but guaranteed.

Okay, perhaps you need a shred of competence. However, most employers are pretty forgiving and allow you to make some mistakes, provided your mistakes don't destroy the company.

On the other hand, workers are keenly aware that if we neglect to show up, we'll quickly be shown the door. Since most of us strive not to live in a refrigerator box, this is excellent motivation.

I don't know about you, but I'd say it's time we give ourselves more credit for showing up. Seriously, it's a significant feat to wake up early, get yourself primped and out the door and on your way to a day of toil. Plus, your boss greatly depends on reliable workers like you. So, a pat on the back is certainly warranted.

From here on out, never let your arrival at work go unnoticed. In fact, feel free to loudly pronounce your arrival each morning. It doesn't matter much what comes out of your mouth, as long as it's loud. Any of these lines would suffice:

- Good morning my fellow lackeys!

- Last night I ate three pounds of uncooked chocolate chip cookie dough!

- Guess who got lucky last night?

Again, management needs people like you, people who are responsible and get to work, day in and day out. If you and your colleagues decided to stop showing up, they'd be royally screwed.

Nice work showing up. Now perhaps you'd like to take a break from reading and go watch a Woody Allen movie.

Stellar Gem #39: Circle Back and Kiss My Ass

Repeat after me and say it slowly: What the fuck are you talking about?

On a typical day at work, I ask myself this question at least 37 times.

In case you haven't been paying attention, there's a pervasive insistence in corporate America to incessantly use made up words, to use nouns as verbs, and to generally butcher the English language. It's hard to take.

The barrage of corporate-speak begins as soon as you come through the door in the morning.

- Hey Jimbo, looks like you have some bandwidth today. Why don't we circle back and take a deeper dive into those numbers?
- In the advertising space, we need to organically grow the business.
- At the end of the day, we need to go after the low-hanging fruit and provide more thought leadership.
- Let's leverage Jill and task her to bring parity to the entire ecosystem.
- Gary, I want you to execute the strategy. (Holy hell. What? You can't murder a helpless strategy. What's wrong with you?)

What do these statements have in common? Bingo! They make people want to stick hot pokers into their ears.

Enough already!

Why do people think it's a good idea to speak this way? Well, I've given this important question three minutes of careful consideration, and I have an answer. I'm convinced people talk this way because, in their minds, it makes them sound smart.

How ironic.

These schmoes may not care that they're confusing and irritating the hell out of the rest of us, but they likely do care about how they are perceived. Therein lies the answer.

For example, let's say you calmly explain to Gary that his corporate speak is driving you nuts. He'll initially be indignant, but I think Gary ultimately yields because he doesn't want you to think he's a tool.

It's time to put an end to this nonsense. Speak plainly. Encourage others to do the same.

Morale at work is bound to improve. In fact, it'll be a win-win-win.

That's right. Count them. That's three wins—50% more wins than the standard "win-win" we've all heard so much about.

Stellar Gem #40: Put 'er There

Shaking hands is kind of a dumb tradition and it spreads germs. The latter point came into sharp focus during the COVID-19 plague.

Google just told me that the handshake goes back almost to the time of Christ. One theory is that warriors shook hands to show they were not concealing weapons and meant no harm to each other. In modern times, handshaking is still used to greet another person or to informally "seal" a deal.

I don't see handshakes going away altogether. That's why I want to pass along my top five rock solid tips for doing it right. Here we go:

1. Never extend your hand with your palm facing down. This says you're arrogant. It's a silent proclamation that you see yourself as dominant and superior. Such a handshake only serves one purpose—to force your co-worker to put out his or her hand palm upward in a submissive fashion.

2. Never extend a limp, lifeless hand. It creeps people out.

3. Never shake someone's hand if your hand is dripping in sweat. I don't care if you're on the verge of a nervous breakdown or you suffer from an odd medical condition, it's disgusting.*

4. Never hold on for dear life. If your handshake lasts longer than it takes to eat a spaghetti dinner, you've held on too long. Shaking someone's hand is not a bull riding contest where the objective hang in there for as long as humanly possible.

5. Never look anywhere except into the other person's eyes. Otherwise, your nickname will be Shifty Bastard, and that's a bad nickname.

If you can abide by my rules, you'll be fine. Unnecessary and unsanitary as the handshake may be, you'll at least be doing it properly.

Someday, maybe the air high-five will gain acceptance at work, and we'll finally be able to keep our nasty germs to ourselves.

---

*Apparently, there is a malady called hyperhidrosis that makes people sweat profusely. Having a name, however, makes it no less disgusting.

Stellar Gem #41: Embrace Shortcuts

What do people have against taking shortcuts? Since I can't hear your answer or, more likely, you're ignoring the question, I'll venture a guess. I'd say people are anti-shortcuts because they wrongly think a shortcut inherently results in shoddy work.

Yes, shortcuts do sometimes lead to things being done half-assed.* However, a shortcut is usually nothing more than a more efficient way of completing a task, and that's exactly the kind of thing that makes your boss happy.

Here's another perk. Shortcuts also help you stay in control of your workload. This leads to less stress and a happier, healthier you.

You surely already know and use shortcuts, like copy and paste. Here are a few you may not have considered:

- Delegate your work to others. You can't do it half-assed if you're not doing it at all. This is also why God made interns. These young and ambitious whipper snappers are eager to please and are basically slaves that never complain.

- Collect every pair of shoes you own with laces. Now walk them to the trash can and throw them in. From now on you'll be wearing loafers. Maybe some Hey Dudes. Or maybe invest in a pair of grandpa shoes. You know, the ones with the Velcro straps. Those are the best and oh so stylish. Plus, you'll never have to stoop over to fiddle with shoelaces again.**

- Never put the cap back on a pen, assuming your pen has a cap. It's a waste of time, like making your bed or putting on pants. There's no telling how many seconds of precious time this could save. As an added bonus, you'll be ready at a moment's notice to scribble down your many genius ideas.

As always, if you dislike any of my suggestions, you can go to hell.

No, I jest. I love you and I sincerely hope adopting more shortcuts will help you feel marginally happier at work.

---

*I'd be sorely disappointed if I find out you were doing your work half-assed. Work should never be done half-assed. Work should always be done—at a minimum—60% assed, unless it's the day before a holiday, in which case just showing up is sufficient.

**You'll also eliminate the risk of tripping on a shoelace, falling down a flight of steps and being forced to wear a full body cast for eight months. You're welcome.

Stellar Gem #42: Be Tenacious

What sorts of things do you pray for? World peace, good health, for God to smite your enemies?

Your prayer habits are none of my business. Nevertheless, I want to suggest you add one more prayer to your repertoire.

Ready?

I want you to ask God to make you more tenacious. And let's hope God answers that one because it's important.

When you want something at work, or anywhere else for that matter, be relentless about going after it and don't to take no for an answer.

For example, I'd like to be financially independent. I'm not there yet, but I will never give up. Never!

With tenacity, you win by wearing people down. I can't give you a timeframe for success, but chances are extremely good you will succeed.

Some of the best ideas are simple ones and this is a perfect example of that. And the best part—even if you haven't been tenacious until now, you can change.

Now I shall share a personal anecdote.

As a young lad, I earned a Bachelor's degree from Temple University. While far from Ivy League, I have nothing but fond memories of the place. Looking back, what I loved (and still do) about the school is the scrappy nature of the students.

Temple is nestled in the badlands of North Philadelphia. The school educates tons of kids from working class backgrounds, many the first in their families to go to college. Few have any sense of entitlement.

I think many of these kids are the picture of tenacity. A lot of them hold part-time jobs to help pay tuition. They put their heads down. They plug away until a degree becomes a reality.

You might not always be the smartest person in the room. Or maybe you'll never be. It's okay. Decide what you want and don't stop until you reach your goal.

WAYS TO MAKE NICE WITH OTHERS

It's amazing there aren't more homicides in the workplace. Not that I would ever condone such a thing. But there's no denying there's a lot of rage in the workplace. Given what workers have to endure, it's understandable.

Still, even though a jury might not convict you, you can't go around killing people. And, no, cutting someone with a broken beer bottle isn't cool either.

With that in mind, I present you with my next pile of gems.

Stellar Gem #43: Stop Being Petty

If you're in a Tom Petty tribute band, don't worry. I would never suggest you quit the band. I love Tom Petty.

If you're part of the rampant pettiness in the workplace, I'm ashamed of you. If Tom Petty was still with us, he'd be ashamed too. Gossip, bickering and office politics at work . . . it's gone on for too long. Here are some things we need to put a stop to:

- Harping on trivial nonsense.

- Withholding information out of spite.

- Eviscerating a perfectly nice co-worker behind his or her back.

- Using passive-aggressive language to push someone's buttons.

- Being a jerk to peers one minute and sweet as sugar to management the next.

It's disheartening.

I guess I shouldn't be too critical of the bad behavior. After all, corporate America has an amazing knack for bringing out the worst in people. Still, if life was fair, petty people would face some kind of negative consequence for their behavior. Seems like they never do though.

Chances are many of these people sit in church pews on Sundays with halos over their heads, like they're Ned Flanders. If they believe in God and an afterlife, maybe they should make more of an effort to curb the pettiness.

All this brings to mind an old bestselling book called *All I Really Need to Know I Learned in Kindergarten*. I never read it but sounds spot on.

Think about it. It's great to know calculus or the names of every U.S. president, but we'd all be better off if we'd go back to what we learned when we were five. Play nicely. Share. Behave. Don't eat glue. Don't pick your nose, or at least don't do it in public.

Starting at an early age, our teachers and parents drilled into us what's most important in life, things like sharing and being kind. So simple, yet many can't remember to live life that way. They allow themselves to be sucked into a black hole of pettiness.

To me, it feels like a very fixable problem.

If you're being petty at work, try not to be. I don't consider myself petty, but I'm not immune, so I'll be mindful as well.

Who knows? Some if it's human nature, but maybe we can squash a lot of it.

Stellar Gem #44: Lighten Up, For the Love of God

When someone makes a mistake at work, I trust no one has been brutally murdered or horribly disfigured. What's more, I suspect the incident hasn't set into motion a series of events that will precipitate the end of the world.

Whew, that's a relief, right?

Now that that's settled, if you're one of these people who always overreact to problems at work, please calm down.

These days, the inability to keep workplace problems in perspective is a colossal problem. In fact, did you know that if people stopped overreacting, we'd reduce the level of depression and anxiety in the workplace by 97.34%?

Yes, that's yet another made-up stat. I'm sorry I lied to you, but I had to get your attention.

Anyone who works can attest to the fact that people are constantly letting their emotions get the better of them. Their greatest strength is spreading stress and anxiety. If they had a motto, it would be: "When you spot a lit candle, hose it down with gasoline." Okay, that's too wordy for a motto, but you get my point.

It's terrible and it leads me to one conclusion—we're taking our jobs far too seriously.

If I'm describing you, you may be thinking:

- Why is this clown judging me?

- Stop picking on me.

- Screw you.

Well, tell your inner voice to pipe down.

To get yourself to lighten up, just remember you'll be dead in 100 years or maybe tomorrow. I'm sorry if that thought throws you into an existential crisis, but that will pass. When it does, thinking of the shortness of life should put those work "emergencies" in the proper perspective.

Most of us don't want to be miserable, so don't be.

Next time the shit hits the fan, don't panic and freak out. Instead, take a deep breath. Then respond with calm and reason and encourage others to do the same. Capisce?

Stellar Gem #45: Win Friends with Chocolate

Let's face it. By and large, Americans are gluttons. All sighted persons know this.

Use this knowledge to win over colleagues.

People will happily scarf down anything put in front of us . . . greasy cheeseburgers, stale crackers, spray cheese, Hot Pockets, a bowl of sugar . . . you name it.

What I've said thus far is fact, like the earth is round or Irish people like beer. So feed your co-workers and you'll win their undying allegiance.

What should you feed them? Chocolate, of course.

Yes, there are many other delicious foods in the world. However, many scrumptious options aren't practical. For example, smothered burritos or BBQ ribs might be a huge hit, but you'd have a huge mess on your hands.

Chocolate, on the other hand, is ideal. More specifically, individually wrapped chocolate candy. I'm clarifying that so you don't leave out a bucket of hot fudge and a ladle.

Chocolate is your best bet because no other food holds the same allure. People can't get enough of it.

If you want to class things up, go out and get yourself a nice candy dish for your desk. Just know that your co-workers don't care about presentation. You could serve the chocolate in your trash can and people would line up to get down on their knees to eat it.

Now, you may be wondering who's going to pay for these sugary treats. Well, I assure you, it won't be me. That leaves you to foot the bill. Of course, you could steal the candy (a.k.a. the five-finger discount), but I can't condone criminal behavior.

Look at it this way. Keeping chocolate at your desk is an investment, but it will pay more dividends than a Warren Buffet stock pick. First, you'll be bringing momentary happiness to people who might be having a bad day. As an added bonus, when you screw up, colleagues will be more forgiving of the infraction as they think back on the delicious sugary bliss you provided.

Finally, when acquiring chocolate, remember—dark chocolate is far superior to milk chocolate. This is not up for debate. And white chocolate is a hell no. Mainly because no one knows for sure what it is. All I know is that it's definitely not chocolate.

Disclaimer: If you scarf down all the treats, you've completely defeated the purpose of this exercise. Please try and show an ounce of self-control next time.

Stellar Gem #46: Go on Mute Genius

True story. I'm in an online meeting. There a couple of dozen other people on the call, including some higher-ups.

Someone on the call, clearly bored and irritated by a couple of the speakers—and thinking she was on mute—chimed in mockingly: "Oh my God! Blah, blah, blah."

I cringe. Did that seriously just happen?

A painfully awkward silence ensues. It maybe lasted seconds, but it felt like an eternity. Then the call continued and everyone acted as if it had never happened.

I didn't recognize the voice, but someone must have. I never found out if she got in trouble for her stupidity. Even if she didn't, she probably did irreparable damage to her reputation.

That was pre-pandemic and, yes, most of us hopefully have gotten much better with video conferencing. But this still seems to be a danger.

Saturday Night Live has done some great skits about the clueless person who does all sorts of inappropriate things while on camera and unmuted. The real-life one seems to be the person who is off camera multi-tasking, making all kinds of distracting noise—and having no idea he's doing it.

Don't be that person.

Now I will end with an explanation of why I almost took out this gem.

Truth be told, I absolutely love when this kind of thing happens. It's tremendously funny.

Despite the entertainment value, I wanted to share this advice because I don't want you to be made fun of or get in trouble. If you slip up and fail to go on mute, you're entitled to a mistake and know that I appreciate your unintentional buffoonery.

Stellar Gem #47: Dial Up the Crazy

Sometime in the near future, it would please me immensely if you'd begin to exhibit some overtly crazy behavior at work.* I think it could lead to greater job satisfaction.

Here are two reasons why:

1. **People will leave you alone.** Is there anything better than to be left alone? No, there's not. Peace and quiet is the best, yet tragically hard to find in the modern work world. So, if its peace and quiet you seek, let people know you're off your rocker.

   If you're stumped on what to do, here are a couple of suggestions:

   Suggestion 1: Periodically mutter curse words for no reason. This will stop any gadfly making a beeline to your cube in his tracks. Your antagonist will then likely begin to stutter and make an awkward retreat. Mission accomplished!

   Suggestion 2: Stare blankly into space. This will yield the same result as Suggestion 1. Just remember that the goal here is not to make people fearful. You don't want them to think you're dangerous or they might call the fuzz.

2. **You'll have more fun.** Once you've laid aside the constraints of sanity, you can be truly free to enjoy yourself more at work.

   Bored? Pretend you're the CEO and show everyone you're in charge by walking around the office like the Queen of England barking orders. Or look someone in the eye and in your most sincere voice say: "Thanks for coming in today."

   Playing the boss is but one example of how you can enjoy the newfound liberation brought about by the removal of your mental health filter.

Soon you'll be having more fun than a barrel of monkeys. Those around you will be having a gay old time as well. They may be laughing with you or they may be laughing at you. Really, what does it matter? You can feel good knowing you gave them a laugh.

Lastly, if any of these antics get you fired, don't try to blame me because I'll act like I don't know you.

---

*I possesses zero psychological credentials, but I did take an Intro to Psychology course once and I think I got a B. Surely that qualifies me to dole out psychological advice. I won't, however, use fancy diagnoses to classify anyone's issue. Instead, I will use my infinitesimal knowledge of psychology to simply label you as either a nut job or normal.

Stellar Gem #48: Show Some Respect

There's one thing we all have in common. No, not an affinity for dressing up like Darth Vader. I'm afraid you're alone on Nerd Island there. What I was referencing is the fact that our time on this earth is finite.

Yep, our days are numbered, which of course is why every second we have is precious. When I waste time, I regret it.* When other people waste my time, it makes me livid.

Sadly, people routinely waste our time, which is one of the big reasons everyone at work is seething with rage below the surface.

Time wasting can take many forms. Here are some examples:

- You're required to go to pointless meetings.

- You show up to a pointless meeting and the person who called the pointless meeting is late.

- Somebody asks you a question they should know the answer to, like "What are we selling again?" or "Where am I?"

- Your employer insists of having fire drills because they think you're too stupid to find your way out of a burning building.

- Harry from accounting keeps whining to you that Linda down the hall keeps refusing to share her phone number because she finds him creepy.

Regardless of why, wasting someone's time is thoughtless, rude, insulting, and I believe in some cultures, punishable by fingernail removal or something equally unpleasant. It's a major violation because lost time can never be reclaimed. It's gone forever, like your virginity.

Another problem is if you're wasting someone else's time and not realizing it. If that's you, knock it off.

If you stop wasting people's time, they'll be eternally grateful. This will lead them to bake cookies for you.

---

*No, I'm not one of those lunatics who always regrets wasting time. Occasional idleness is not only okay, it's necessary. If you don't believe me, it's only because you've been brainwashed by our workaholic culture.

Stellar Gem #49: Pat Someone on the Back

When someone does a nice job at work, does confetti drop from the ceiling? Does Queen's *We Are the Champions* start blaring from speakers all over the office?

No.

Screw up, however, and it's guaranteed people will notice. Probably with some negative consequences, perhaps a good old fashioned public flogging or revocation of toilet privileges.

Why are so many ready to pounce on you when you mess up while positive contributions go unnoticed and unappreciated?

Not cool.

It's no mystery workers feel unhappy. In fact, did you know that each day 18.4 million Americans walk around feeling dejected because no one recognizes their hard work?*

If you can relate, I might have a solution.

That solution can be summed up in the words of Mahatma Gandhi or whoever said: *"Be the change you want to see in the world."* Yes, it does sounds like a bumper sticker, but hey, it's true and a beautiful sentiment.

You have the power to make the world better place with small acts of kindness. So go ahead and pat someone on the back once in a while for a job well done.**

I don't want to get all kumbaya here, but thoughtful acts brighten other people's day. That, in turn, will put you in a better mood. I know. It's so simple and obvious.

Make someone else's day a little brighter and your day automatically gets brighter too.

*I don't know why I feel compelled to keep making up phony statistics. It never ends. From here on out, you should assume I'm full of it.

**Under no circumstances should you actually touch anyone's back, or any other body part for that matter. That sort of thing in our litigious society will surely end badly for you, so no touching!

Stellar Gem #50: Pee Silently

This gem is aimed (he-he) at my male readers. Makes sense if you consider that the bulk of my urinating experiences have taken place in men's rooms.*

Ladies, don't feel excluded. You may still find this edifying.

First, let's review some male urination basics.

When a guy needs to take a whiz, he heads to the men's bathroom.

With me so far? Good.

Now, once inside the loo, said male with the full bladder is presented with a wall of urinals. At this point, the guy chooses a urinal and, ah, merciful relief!

This relief, however, can come at a price.

While the pee is flowing, there's always a risk some nudnick will saunter up to the urinal next to the one you're using, which in and of itself is a violation since you are always supposed to leave at least one buffer urinal between you and the other urinator, whenever possible. Then, to make matters worse, the nudnick will initiate some inane chit-chat.

Yep. There you are, trying to take care of business, when your new buddy starts yammering. It often will start with a question, perhaps:

- How about that game last night?

- Seen any good movies lately?

- Are you circumcised?

It's annoying, so if you're one of these people, consider yourself on notice.

Until co-workers learn this lesson, you can use a stall. Or even wearing adult diapers would be an improvement.

Longer term, I may have an entrepreneurial idea to eradicate the problem.

I'm going to start a bathroom monitoring company. Other companies will pay me a lot of moolah to send over Urinal Attendants. The ideal candidate for the job would be someone with experience as a librarian and a Navy Seal.

The Urinal Attendant will loudly shush anyone who violates the strict "No Talking" rule. To reinforce the importance of silence, we'll hang signs that say "Zip it!" This will serve two purposes: (1) It will serve as a friendly reminder to be quiet, and (2) it's also a cheeky nudge to zip your pants when finished. If the urinator refuses the Urinal Attendant will then snap the offender's neck like a twig.

Clearly another phenomenal idea by me. By the way, I'm going to need considerable capital to get this off the ground. Since I'm sure you'll want to get in on it, I'll be in touch soon to get your routing number.

*I do have considerable experience peeing outside. It's the best part of being a guy, which I suppose is sad.

Stellar Gem #51: Learn from Art the Fart

When I was a kid, there was a cantankerous old man who lived across the street. I don't remember his last name. His first name was Arthur, or Art for short.

Unfortunately for him, Art rhymes with fart.* It wasn't long before this dawned on some of the neighborhood kids and a new nickname was born: Art the Fart.

As you might imagine, grumpy old Art didn't take kindly to his new nickname. In fact, I can't overstate how much it pissed him off.

Art would regularly demonstrate this displeasure by yelling and, in a low energy way, briefly chasing whichever kid(s) vocalized the nickname in his presence. To the best of my knowledge, Art never caught anyone.**

Was Art entitled to get angry? Sure. I bet Art had his share of problems in life just like the rest of us. He certainly didn't need added grief from punk kids.

Art's major slip-up, however, was how he handled these situations. Chasing the neighbor kids was, hands down, the worst way to deal with the problem.

Why? Because getting old Art riled up was the whole point of the exercise. His reactions had the opposite effect. They delighted his antagonists.

If only Art could have been stoic. If only he didn't let on that that dumb nickname bothered him, kids would have quickly lost interest and turned their attention to looking for beer or a stray cat to torture.

Odds are good your name isn't Art, and even if it is, chances are no one is taunting you. But there's a lot passive-aggressive behavior in the workplace. Grown men and women, allegedly professional, who get off on goading people, pushing their buttons—and lots of people take the bait.

If this happens to you, take the high road. Whether the person is trying to make you angry or to make you cry is irrelevant. Never to play into their hands. Don't give them the satisfaction.

Also, if you have a first names like Art, Nick, or Tucker, you may want to consider a name change.

---

*When my son was in preschool, he introduced me to "butt burp," an excellent synonym for fart. Please feel free to use it.

**You're clearly wondering if I ever taunted Art. Well, I can honestly say no, I did not. That's not to say I could always keep from laughing if I witnessed one of the chases.

Stellar Gem #52: Be Young and Good Looking

Years ago, 60 Minutes ran a fascinating segment that highlighted the power of being young and good looking. The show's producers conducted an experiment with two types of people: beautiful and homely. The experiment put actors in common life situations to see who fared better.

In one test, two women took turns standing on the side of the road, pretending to have car trouble. One was young and hot. The other wasn't. Both were looking for a Good Samaritan willing to stop and help.

You guessed it.

Probably more out of horniness than kindness, the hottie quickly had multiple offers to help (from men naturally). And, yes, the less attractive woman was left stranded.

More surprisingly these biases also held true for men. Cameras rolling, the TV network sent two actors into a job interview and the results were the same. The less handsome guy, even with a clearly superior resume, got passed over for the job. The less qualified but taller, better dressed, better looking dude was offered the job.

What can be done about all this?

Make the most of the cards you've been dealt.

Thankfully this is the 21st century and there never have been more options to improve our appearance:

- **If you're only mildly repugnant and decrepit.** Proceed to your neighborhood drug store. Then go down each aisle and load up on every beauty enhancing product you can lay your hands on.

  Here's a partial shopping list: teeth whitener, mouthwash, hair dye, anti-acne medicine, make up (not recommended for men), nail file, lotions, loofah, dandruff shampoo, conditioner, tweezers, hair spray, and fake tanner.

- **If you're acutely ugly and decrepit.** You still want to buy all of the aforementioned crap, but you'll have to kick it up a notch. Once you leave your neighborhood drugstore, proceed to the nearest cosmetic surgeon for some more radical enhancements. Restore that hair, eliminate those wrinkles, fix those teeth . . . there's no limit to what modern surgery can offer.

Yes, you're beautiful on the inside. That doesn't, however, mean you can ignore your outside.

All kidding aside, I'd like to end with a plea. Asian people, by and large, genuinely value the elderly and their wisdom. In America and other Western nations, not so much. It's not easy getting old, so can we please show our elders more respect?

Stellar Gem #53: Pucker Up Baby

I think you know where I'm headed. That's right Chester. It's time to talk about the art of ass kissing.

Did you know that ass kissing has been around as long as people have had asses? Your job is to master this ancient art form, so pucker up. When you do, your career will flourish.

Just like a virtuoso pianist, mastering the art form takes serious commitment and diligent practice. Since you have to walk before you can run, let's review the fundamentals.

Ass kissing 101

What's the secret to being good at this? It's quite simple. The main thing you need to remember it's all about flattery. I mean, who doesn't love a compliment every now and then?

That's right, we all love it. You're brilliant!

See what I mean? I bet that compliment felt nice.

Flattery will get you far in life. Make other people feel good and they'll return the favor by helping you on your journey. This might take the form of a co-worker stepping in to help you with a difficult assignment. Or the person you complimented might decide to share her delicious gourmet cupcakes with you.

When dispensing flattery, it's crucial to convey sincerity. If you come across as insincere, you've wasted your time.

If you're not a natural at this, I'm afraid you'll need to practice extra hard. I don't like things that require effort either, but I fear that's the way it is.

Now, think of a list of compliments you can use at work. Then practice saying them in front of a mirror. To get the ball rolling, I've selflessly come up with a few samples compliments you may feel to use:

- Boy Gary, that sure is a stunningly nice shirt you have on today!

- Gertrude, is it just me or have you been hitting the gym? You could bounce a tennis ball off those abs!

- I hope you don't mind me saying so, but that PowerPoint presentation was a delight!

- Has anyone told you that you look a lot like *[insert name of your favorite hot actress/actor]*!

- You know, I think you're the smartest person I've ever met!

- I didn't even know you could purchase eyeglass frames that sharp looking!

You get the drift.

Once you're feeling confident, get into the office and start unleashing a torrent of compliments, and you might want to lay it on thick with management since they control all the money.

Stellar Gem #54: Quit Your Whining

I admit I like to whine. It's fun. It's cathartic. And it's out of control at work.

Before I share my ingenious plan to curb the whining, allow me tell you why it bothers me. No, you didn't ask, but I can't let that stop me.

It bothers me because I think our ancestors would be deeply ashamed of us.

You no doubt have legit complaints, but whatever is getting under your skin, look to the past for some perspective. Unlike the old days, you probably won't have to put in exceedingly long hours, slaving away until you keel over and die. So, there's that.

Past and present, the list of jobs worse than yours is long. Here are a few:

- Leech collector

- Coal miner

- Asbestos worker

- Executioner

- Food taster (you know, the person who had to try the king's food to make sure it wasn't poisoned)

Furthermore, when you catch yourself complaining too much on the job, remind yourself of your high standard of living. Before you disagree, I'd like to point out that you're likely living like a king compared to our ancestors.

Nowhere is our sweet standard of living more apparent than with food. Stores open 24 hours a day, 365 days a year; supermarkets filled with a jaw-dropping number of choices (How many Oreo flavors do we really need?); and tons of good meal options already cooked or that can be cooked in minutes with your microwave.

Don't even get me started on the long list of absurd luxuries we enjoy. I spent a few minutes thinking about my stuff and came up with these items which I'm borderline embarrassed to own:

- Stamps I don't need to lick.

- A car that turns on with without a key and heated leather seats because, God forbid, my ass gets a chill.

- Clothes that don't wrinkle.

- About a billion TV options.

- And, of course, the mother of all unnecessary luxuries: The ability to buy anything my mind can think of in seconds and have it delivered nearly as fast.

Yet are we happy? Nooooo.

Whining may be human nature and it can feel good, but let's rein it in.

Stellar Gem #55: Mind Your Microwave Manners

Unless your office is a total Greek tragedy, it has a break room. That break room has at least one microwave oven (so the slaves can quickly warm up leftovers, scarf them down, and get back to toiling).

Microwaves are a modern marvel and, gosh darn it, I love them.* Sure, they're probably slowly but surely giving us all cancer, but boy can they heat a burrito in no time!

Alas, it's not all good though.

What I've decided to harp on next is the fact that a lot of people refuse to adhere to the most basic microwave etiquette. The #1 infraction—reheating foul-smelling food.

Here are some examples:

- Jimmy pops a piece of cod fish into the old nuker. He cranks that baby up and soon it's like a mustard gas attack, nauseated colleagues doubled-over everywhere you look.

- Megan's in the mood for some microwave popcorn. Won't that be nice? No Megan. It's not nice because you're inept. It's not okay to microwave the kernels 5x longer than recommended, permeating the air with the nostril-offending smell of burnt popcorn.

- Boy, does Jenny the vegan love her organic, humane, locally grown broccoli, cabbage, and weird root vegetables. Too bad she's the only one. Hey, Jenny, you're already annoying people by being vegan. Don't make it worse.

What do all these people have in common?

Yes, they're rude and inconsiderate.

If you have bad microwave manners, I bet you do better at home. You probably say "thank you" when someone passes the mashed potatoes and "excuse me" when you let one rip after your third serving of refried beans. That means you're almost there. All you have to do is start bringing that same mindset to your place of employment. If you don't, people will ostracize you and you will feel sad.

By the way, you might be wondering why I didn't single out Indian food as a no-no for the microwave. I suppose I should have because I know some find the odor repulsive, but I love it. Plus, I can only assume it's not bothering any Indian colleagues. But yea, still might better to save that tandoori chicken for home.

---

*I have to admit that I lack even a rudimentary understanding of how anything works. In fact, unless it was invented circa 1700, I honestly have no clue how it operates. The microwave oven is merely one example of this. Computers, remote controls, radios, engines, digital cameras, bread that never gets stale. It's all black magic to me.

Stellar Gem #56: Stop Eating Shit Sandwiches

Who ordered the shit sandwich?

Hmm, not me. Did you? No, I didn't think so. And why would you? A shit sandwich is an unreasonable task wrapped in a bogus "opportunity."

Okay then. The next time someone puts such a sandwich in front of you at work—don't eat it!

If you want to be happy at work, sometimes you're going to have to assert yourself. That's not a green light to be an idiot. Just stand up for yourself and it will be fine. The negative consequences of standing up for yourself at work are largely imagined.

Plus, who knows? If you assert yourself in the right way, the person offering you the sandwich may walk away with a newfound respect for you. Or, at the very least, he or she may think twice before offering you a smelly delicacy in the future.

You must also never allow colleagues to pass off the sandwich as something else. For example, someone may try to trick you by telling you that it's is really a scrumptious chicken salad on a warm focaccia roll. The server might also point out that it comes with a pickle. Do not be deceived!

Why are these sandwiches always on the menu? I think it stems from the fact that there are no problems at work, only "opportunities."

Usually, a bogus work opportunity is mainly a surefire way to increase your stress level, lose sleep, gain weight, get heartburn, raise your blood pressure, and lose lots of quality time with your loved ones—all in an effort to try and diffuse some bomb at work.

Then, when you step in and heroically steer the corporation away from tragedy, you're unlikely to be any better off financially and you won't feel warm and fuzzy inside.

Stick with the traditional sandwiches like ham and cheese or peanut butter and jelly.

Stellar Gem #57: Stay Away from Other People's Lunches

Speaking of sandwiches, the last gem reminds me of my all-time favorite work email.

The email came from corporate security. I don't remember verbatim what it said, but I'll give you the gist.

It had come to security's attention that someone had been helping themselves to other people's lunches. Security was alerting us that they were on top of the situation and that the perpetrator should stop at once, or face the consequences.

Of course, I found the whole asinine situation highly amusing. I mean, the thought of someone lurking about, rifling through the office fridge until he (let's face it, it had to be a guy) happened upon something irresistible.

You can't make this stuff up.

Maybe even funnier was that some Barney Fife (or a whole squad of them) was on the case.* Another surreal day at the cubicle farm.

Is this sort of theft commonplace? It wouldn't surprise me if it is.

Who knows? Maybe you've perpetrated such a culinary crime. Maybe you're even scheming to do this tomorrow. If so, I fear your life has veered terribly off course.

You also know better. Taking someone else's food is stealing and that's wrong, not to mention pathetic.

In case you're curious, I'm not sure our crack security team ever apprehended the culprit. So, be careful out there. That sandwich thief could still be on the prowl—and surely hungry. He could be eyeing your lunch right now.

---

*If you're some young whipper snapper, you may not know that Barney Fife was a comically inept character on The Andy Griffith Show played by the very talented Don Knotts. He was a great TV character, so if you get a chance, check out an episode on YouTube.

Stellar Gem #58: Eat the Breath Mint

From time to time, someone at work will offer you a mint (or a piece of gum). When this happens, you must always say thank you and eat it. No exceptions.

Your breath might smell like a lovely bouquet of spring flowers or an overpriced Yankee Candle. Or it might smell like a mixture of sour milk and cat pee.

Unless you've just brushed your teeth, you don't really know what your breath smells like. So, again, forget about whether you or not you want the mint. Just eat the damn breath mint.

That's all I can say on this topic. Yet I feel I've shortchanged you with this gem and that saddens me. Therefore, I shall continue writing about a related topic.

Now that I've addressed your halitosis, I'll use this space to confront another socially embarrassing stank issue—excessive perfume and cologne and after-shave.

Personally, I never use the stuff, although I do own a bottle of cologne. It has to be at least 20 years old and the bottle is still 98% full. And no, I can't explain why I haven't thrown it away.

While I never took to the stuff, I won't stand in your way if you wish to wear some, even at work. But I draw the line at bathing in the stuff.

Please use it sparingly. It's potent stuff. A dab or two is plenty. If you're bathing in it, you've gone too far.

Why do people have such a hard time with this? My theory is that people who lather it on before heading into the office are under a delusion that it will make them irresistible to hot co-workers. They fantasize that it's all going to lead to some kind of erotic session in the office supply closet with a co-worker.

Perfume, cologne or after-shave, when applied liberally, makes people gag. People don't like to gag and thus will become agitated and openly hostile toward you. If it gets really bad, a colleague who can't take it any more will dump a bucket of soapy water on you to remedy the situation.

If you can't quit cold turkey, I beseech you to start tapering off your daily dousing. If, you're going through a gallon of perfume a week, maybe get that down to a half gallon, then a pint, then I don't know, maybe 1/100 of an ounce.

Now go take a shower. I can smell you from here.

Stellar Gem #59: Take Your Phlegm Elsewhere

What's the grossest word in the English language? Hard to say. I'd say phlegm has to be near the top of the list though.

Merely hearing or seeing that word makes me queasy. That's because it conjures up a vile image of thick, oozing mucus, not quite green and not quite yellow. Quick, somebody get me a trash can. I'm going to hurl.

Now, as for you, you can't be wandering into work hacking up phlegm. It's a serious violation, and not only because it's gross. You're also being an inconsiderate jerk who's sending the message that you don't care about the health of the people around you.

When you're sick, even if there's not a raging pandemic, why not stay home? Seriously, it's not a badge of honor to drag yourself to the office.

If you don't stay home, your colleagues will surmise that you have a total disregard for their welfare. Then they will make little voodoo dolls of you and stick them with pins. Is that what you want?

Coming into work sick is also perplexing given how much you hate work. Why wouldn't you jump at the chance to stay home?

Part of me wants to cut you some slack if you go to work sick. After all, our free-market economy leaves millions feeling deeply financially insecure and fearful of job loss. Call out sick, and for some, there can be negative consequences.

I hope the converse isn't happening—that anyone thinks they're too important to miss a day or two of work due to illness. The hard truth is that we're all expendable and your employer can chug along just fine without you.

Again, do the rest of us a favor and stay home the next time you're under the weather. It's the right thing to do and you'll enjoy it.

Make the most of being home too. As Dorothy from the Wizard of Oz famously said, there's no place like it. Lie around in your silk bathrobe (I know you have one), take a nap, eat some chicken noodle soup, and mindlessly watch hours of your favorite TV shows.

And don't worry. You'll be feeling better and back to working for the man in no time.

Stellar Gem #60: Practice Prempathy

Customers want to know that you care about them. The only problem is, you don't.

Don't worry. I'm not here to make you feel guilty about your callousness, and never fear; your icy cold heart need not hamper your quest to be happier at work, thanks to prempathy.

What is prempathy? Don't waste your time looking elsewhere for a definition because it's made up. Hey George W. Bush used made up words all the time. Why can't I?

Prempathy means, as you may have guessed, pretend empathy.

While this word can be used in a variety of situations, it's most appropriate in the customer service world.

If you're still scratching your head about what the hell I'm prattling on about, allow me to clarify with an example. The following is hypothetical conversation between a call center representative and an obnoxious customer:

Customer Service Rep: Thank you for calling Dewey Cheetam and Howe Enterprises. How may I be of service to you today?

Customer: Yes, I purchased your lousy pet food for my pedigreed cat, Rolex. Well, Rolex isn't happy.

Customer Service Rep: Oh no, that's terrible! I'm sorry to hear that. Poor Rolex! Rest assured, we'll do whatever it takes to make Rolex happy.

Customer: You damn well better if you know what's good for you! Mark my words, you people will be hearing from my lawyers!

Customer Service Rep: Of course. It's been an absolute pleasure speaking with you. Thank you for calling.

Now go give it a try. By this time next week, it should be an integral part of your work life.

Stellar Gem #61: Cozy Up to a Colleague

Given the inordinate amount of time people spend with co-workers, you'd think we'd all know each other intimately. Yet often we don't take time out to get to know one another. All the talk is about work, work, and more work.

Heavy workloads in many places don't allow for idle chit-chat. In these places, you pass someone in the hall, you might say a few words to one another in passing. Or, if that's too much exertion, maybe words are supplanted by a head nod.

Granted, if you take time to get to know someone, you may wish you hadn't. But let's not be pessimistic. For every person who turns out to be a jerk or a nut job, you'll surely find someone you genuinely like and find interesting. Heck, you might even meet your new best buddy. Better yet, if you're single, you could wind up with more than a friend, if you catch my drift (wink-wink, cha-ching).

Of course, I'm a hypocrite. None of this comes easy to me. I'm a quiet person, a true introvert, someone who likes to keep his cards close to his vest, even though I don't own a vest. I also tend to put my head down so I can get the work done and flee at 5 p.m.

It's not that I don't have interest in the lives of others. I do. The issue is that I cherish my time outside of work and chit-chat often results in having to work late to make up for the time lost. I'm trying to do better though.

What about you? Are you willing to put in some effort to get to know your co-workers better?

It's fine if you're not a great conversationalist. People are obsessed with themselves, so simply ask questions that center on them and won't be able to get a word in edgewise. Just listen and grunt or nod your head or repeat back something they say.

CAUTION: Beware of bad icebreakers

There's virtually no limit to the questions you might ask a co-worker to break the ice. Others you will want to avoid, like:

- Hey, what's your credit score?

- Does anyone else in your family have a unibrow?

- Cat hoarder. Am I right?

- Can you recommend a good hemorrhoidal cream?

A small sample. I'm sure you could think of others.

Now go be social and leave me alone.

Stellar Gem #62: Give in to Your Hero Cravings

Yes, by all means, go enjoy a delicious hero sandwich if your stomach desires one.* I'll wait here.

What's that? No thank you, I already ate.

When you finish your meal, you should be energized and laser focused on learning all about the *real* gem—giving in to your desire to be a bona fide hero, and not a sandwich kind. Think Mother Theresa, George Washington, Jonas Salk, or Batman (but not Aquaman because he's lame).

How do I know you want to be a hero?

Well, I didn't use my psychic powers, although I think we both know I could if I wanted to. No, the reason I know you want to be a hero is simple. Deep down we all want that for two reasons:

1. People fawn over heroes and that's awesome, especially if you're trying to attract a mate.

2. Hero status allows you to pretty much do whatever you want.

In a nutshell, that's why you want to be a hero. Now let's discuss what constitutes a hero.

For some, a hero rescues people from burning buildings or cures disease. But then there's also the less noble form of heroism, like hitting a drunk double in a bar league softball game or winning a competitive eating contest.

I make these distinctions because being a traditional hero is a lofty goal. And, if you're anything like me, you don't have the energy for that.

Work is depleting enough. So, let's not worry about knocking the ball out of the park. Instead take it down 12 notches and tackle these smaller feats of heroism at work:

- **Rain contingency gear (code for umbrellas).** Keeping a spare umbrella handy can win you mucho brownie points, especially if it's rainy and cold. You can also post a sign that "Rain Contingency Gear" so folks know you're open to sharing and not some weird umbrella hoarder.

- **Bring in donuts.** Drive to the donut store. Buy donuts. Offer them to your co-workers. I trust you don't have questions.

- **Think of your own ideas.** Seriously, I give and give. You can't expect me to do all the work.

In conclusion, as I've astutely outlined, you have the power to turn your hero dreams into reality. All it takes is some solid, half-assed effort.

---

*If you ever visit Philly and order a "hero" sandwich, you might get punched in the face. The word you want is hoagie. If you really want to sound local, say it this way: "Yo, can I get a hoagie over here or what?" Note that this is a rhetorical question. You will always get your hoagie.

Stellar Gem #63: Stop Acting Like a Smacked Ass

What exactly is a smacked ass?

Very good question. The first thing you need to know is that there are two flavors: people who act like jerks and people who are arrogant. Or sometimes it's a combo—an arrogant jerk.

Regrettably, some can't help themselves. It's who they are. It would be easier to have them change their height or the number of times they look in the mirror than change their ways. It's in their DNA.

That's not you or me though. We're genuinely nice people. Under stress, however, it's possible for even good eggs like us to turn rotten and exhibit this kind of behavior from time to time.

That's why you should try to police yourself at work. If you don't, you could gain a reputation as a smacked ass and your career will crater.

Oh, you'll also have no friends. Don't want to overlook that.

The good news is you already know what to do to turn it around. It's all stuff your mom taught you. If you treated someone badly, say you're sorry. That sort of thing.

Unfortunately, technology has made it tremendously easy to mistreat one another. Email, text messages and social media make it a snap to be mean and arrogant from a distance.

We send tons of messages to co-workers. Even if you can't be nice 100% of the time, at least try and refrain from being snarky. I know you think you're hilarious, but trust me. We're all weary of the snark.

Also, you can avoid the label if you practice some humility. Stay humble, without being a doormat, and people will like you. Start to get cocky, however, and you'll deservedly be disliked.

By the way, big deal if you are the smartest or best-looking person in the room. Those are gifts from the big man upstairs, so don't be so full of yourself.

Lastly, when you're up in heaven or burning in the big cubicle farm down below, do you want those you left behind to say something nice about you, like "Boy, that Gary sure was a prince!"? Or would you prefer: "That Gary, what a smacked ass he was!"

Stellar Gem #64: Cure That Diarrhea of the Mouth

Writing has been my bread and butter for decades. Yes, that makes me a geezer, although I don't see why you had to point that out.

As is true with many writers, and as I've stated before, I'm an introvert. Being an introvert isn't a bad thing. Yet introverts, from an early age, regularly receive both subtle and not so subtle messages that we're inferior.

It's absurd, and the vast biases against introverts show up in a lot of ways, like extroverts constantly saying idiotic things like "Don't be shy." or to "Come out of your shell."*

Meanwhile, God forbid an introvert ask an extrovert to stop talking because their blathering on is excruciatingly annoying. Hey, guess what? You don't have to vocalize every thought that bubbles up in your brain. A lot of it really isn't all that interesting. Start trying to see the beauty in peace and quiet.

If you are constantly unleashing a verbal assault on those around you, you have an ailment. More specifically, you have diarrhea of the mouth.**

Unlike most illnesses, the person with diarrhea of the mouth feels fine. It's the people within earshot who suffer.

Maybe you already have some self-awareness about your condition or maybe this diagnosis comes as news to you. Either way, you need to know that you're making people's ears bleed with your prattle, so it's time to talk less.

Don't bother heading to your local pharmacy either. You can search the shelves all you want. You won't find a pill that will remedy this problem. It's all on you to exercise some self-control.

Give it two weeks. If the diarrhea hasn't abated, stick a sock in it. Literally. Go find a sock, a long one, roll it up and stuff it in your mouth.

*Newsflash: Most introverts are not afraid to talk. Introverts prefer to think things over before speaking. What a concept!

**My dad had a rolodex of crass, fun sayings I (mostly) remember fondly and I pulled "diarrhea of the mouth" from that rolodex. While I'm thinking about it, here is a short list of other Bill Steadman classics, with a little history and instruction, where applicable, on how you too can use them:

- *"It's a little warm for Christmas."* Appropriate any time you're asked to open your wallet or purse. It doesn't really matter if it's warm or not, although it may cause confusion on cold days in December.

- *"The blue urine."* This is a reference to the ocean that seemed to crop up later in dad's life. I'm pretty certain you'll never have a use for it. My dad loved the ocean, but mostly looking at it from a beach. The early years of his were lived by the sea in Ireland and he spent his working years as a radio officer in the U.S. Merchant Marine, where he'd be away for several weeks at a time. I guess that got old.

- *"Wow, now there's a heavy hitter."* This refers to an obese person not someone who can knock the cover off of a baseball. When his mind was crippled by dementia, this one would slip out—a lot—while we had breakfast at a restaurant that was typically crawling with heavy hitters.

- *"It doesn't owe you anything."* Both practical and reassuring. If a material possession served you well and you have to break down and buy a new one, so be it.

Stellar Gem #65: Listen Up

I said, listen up! Geez, get the wax out of your ears.

Since the last gem was about talking less, seems only appropriate to turn our attention to being a better listener.

Some seem to think hearing and listening as the same thing. Not true. The main difference is listening requires effort.

You know by now that I don't like things that are difficult. I want life to be easy, like a walk in the park or pie.*

Not listening has negative consequences in all aspects of our lives. At work, if you listen poorly, you can get yourself into all kinds of trouble. Here are a few examples:

- Jennifer from marketing, sick of reminding you that you're not her type, finally follows through on getting that restraining order.

- You accidentally agree to bake four dozen cupcakes for the department pot luck.

- You're let go after the boss catches you with a half-dressed co-worker in the supply closet. (Maybe daydreaming during the professional conduct training video wasn't the best idea.)

Well, don't worry. Once again, I'm here to help.

Given I just offered to help you become a better listener, I could see how you might conclude that I must be a great listener. Yea, not really.

I used to think I was a terrific listener. Then I got married and my spouse set the record straight, pointing out many examples of less-than-optimal listening skills.

The good news is that I've gotten marginally better at listening—and you can too.

My problem is that I sometimes zone out when people talk. It's not that I don't want to listen. I do. It's just that, well, I get bored with a lot people have to say and I start daydreaming.

It's hard not to get defensive when someone accuses you of being a bad listener. In the past, I'd be taken aback and think: "Hey pal, maybe if you had something more interesting to say, I'd hang on every word."

Overall, though, I'd say the whole listening business is going better for me. These days I'll listen to almost anyone . . . dullards, geeks, weirdoes, criminals, Civil War reenactors . . . you name it.

The bottom line is I've heard a bunch of smart people say listening is important. So, like it or not, you gotta try.

---

*I get the walk in the park saying, but I fail to see what could even be remotely easy about making pie. At the risk of sounding like a braggard, I'm pretty phenomenal at eating pie, but making one? No clue. Unless I can count throwing a frozen Mrs. Smith's into the oven.

Stellar Gem #66: Put the Dumb Smartphone Down

It's a good thing our phones are smart because, as far as I can tell, a lot of people carrying them are morons.

Now I must warn you that I'm about to launch into a rant. So, put the book down and run if you must.

My rant springs from the fact that I'm a bit of a technology curmudgeon. To keep things positive, however, you can call me something kinder. Let's go with "late adopter."

Technology frequently irritates me. Nowhere is this more evident than in the world of smartphones.

Don't get me wrong. I've been tremendously impressed by all the tech the Silicon Valley nerd billionaires have created. Those are some seriously clever nerds. Nevertheless, thinking about it as a consumer, I feel we've all been duped.

Marketers have convinced billions of us that social media and screens are as vital as oxygen. Of course, they never acknowledge the huge downside, things like:

- Compulsive checking for inane updates from your cyber-friends. Oh, you had a fish taco for lunch? That's so interesting. Oh wait, no it's not!

- Dead-eyed staring at a computer screen while ignoring the human being standing right in front of you.

- Being so absorbed in your device that you fail to notice the natural beauty around you or outside your window, when you're stuck working indoors.

- Endless monthly payments to help ensure lower-income people continue to live hand to mouth.

This isn't to say I don't see the upside. Smartphones are amazing and I'm grateful to have one. They're cool, useful, and fun. Plus, when you're trying to earn a living, you can get quite a lot of work done with a smartphone.

There is one misconception I feel needs clearing up. Owning a smartphone isn't a lifetime pass to being obnoxious.

Smartphones are here to stay, or at least until the tech companies start surgically implanting the next generation of computers into our bodies. Don't worry, that will be here soon. After that, the robots will be in charge and we'll quickly be 100% enslaved.

While we wait for that happy day, if you have bad smartphone habits and can acknowledge it, that's a great first step. Then you can dial back your offensive smartphone behavior a little.

It will be hard at first because you're addicted, but it will get easier. Ultimately, it will all be worth it because fewer people will call you a schmuck.

Stellar Gem #67: Curb "Reply to All"

Working for the man is like living in a Dilbert cartoon. The "reply to all" email option is a great example.

The early pioneers of electronic mail created the "reply to all" feature specifically to bring out the buffoon in us—and they succeeded in a big way.

Here's an asinine scenario that's played out over and over at companies around the country. Names have been changed to protect the stupid.

John sends an email and includes a large group that should not have gotten the message. Sandy, confused by the email, hits "reply to all" and says: "I'm not familiar with this project. I think you sent this to me by mistake."

Approximately 180 other perplexed co-workers follow suit, each one asking to be taken off the mail list.

At this point, Gary, who is about to have an aneurism, sends out a note testily asking everyone to please stop hitting "reply to all."

Then 76 people who didn't read Gary's note send out their own emails asking to be taken off of John's mail list.

John replies to each of these individuals, and hits "reply to all," apologizing for his mistake and providing assurances the error won't happen again.

Then 32 people hit "reply to all" after getting John's note to thank him for taking care of the problem. John replies to these individuals, and copies everyone, to let people know they are welcome.

Not to be outdone, 26 people hit "reply to all" to convey that they hope John enjoys his weekend. John, eager to have the last word, hits "reply to all" to say "You too."

Gary and several other aggravated employees proceed to shoot themselves in the head.

Okay, maybe that's an exaggeration, but it's not that far off and it's confounding. These chowderheads have college degrees.

Sending an email to the right people isn't difficult. Truly, it's not. I don't know if people are daydreaming, moving too fast, or smoking too many doobies. Regardless, there's no excuse.

All you have to do is take a few seconds to make sure you're emailing the right people before you hit send. So simple. You'll save yourself a lot of embarrassment and no one will have to shoot themselves in the head.

WAYS TO MAKE NICE WITH OTHERS

Laughter is the best medicine. Well, drugs are better, but I think we can all agree humor is tremendously important.

After joining the labor market, a young adult will realize, most likely within the first ten minutes, that corporate America is largely a humorless desert.

I realize we can't be perpetually amused at work. That's why they call it work and not fun. Nevertheless, what do you say we try to take on this problem?

Great. Glad you're onboard.

Setting a goal to increase amusement at work is a commendable goal. My next 15 gems are designed to help us do that.

Stellar Gem #68: Stick to Non-mandated Fun

You like to have fun. I like to have fun. We all like to have fun. However, as Dr. Suess once wrote "It is fun to have fun, but you have to know how."*

What's seldom fun is when management instructs us to have fun.

Few things will elicit a collective groan more than a managerial invitation to partake in some good old-fashioned, forced socializing. Yet these events persist, organized by people who are undeterred by bad cake and awkward conversation. This is all brilliantly depicted in the birthday cake scene in the movie Office Space.**

Time and again, management insists on organizing "fun" events for us. "Let's show these worker bees how benevolent we are. Let's herd them into a sterile conference room with bad florescent lighting, prohibit music and booze, and let the good times roll?"

I've been to a few that were very painful. Painful like undergoing a root canal while being waterboarded.

At this point, you can dismiss me as an anti-social nut, but I do generally like people. And I love good camaraderie with co-workers. It's very special to have colleagues who care and look out for one another. I think that stuff happens naturally though.

So, what should you do when you get invited to an event you don't want to attend?

Well, you need to get creative. Tell them you have to wash your hair, or that your parakeet broke its leg and you need to take her to physical therapy.

You have my blessing to spin whatever tale you like.

Lastly, instead of a karaoke sing-a-long, I know a surefire way to boost morale. It's a beautiful four-letter word: cash. Extra vacation days can also work wonders.

---

*Yes, that line is from Cat in the Hat! Nice work.

**For shame if you've never seen Office Space. Make sure you read Gem #96.

Stellar Gem #69: Milk the Baby

Wow, do I really need to clarify that if you have a baby, you should never try to extract milk from it? That would be certifiable and probably a felony.

I bring up babies because they possess a super power. A baby will work miracles if you bring one to your place of employment. That's because a sweet little baby will have people grinning like idiots and making nonsensical noises that, quite frankly, will likely scar the child for life.

But, don't worry. The damage to your child's psyche will be worth it.

Why?

For starters, you'll feel good for having brightened someone's day. More importantly, since you did them a solid, they will be hugely indebted to you.

Don't have a baby? Okay, that's a bit of a hurdle, but don't let that stop you.

You must know someone who has a baby. And I doubt it would be hard to convince those harried parents to loan the kid to you for a few hours. In fact, if you play your cards right, the parents might even pay you.

Before I go any further, let me acknowledge that a screaming infant isn't endearing.

That's why you need to make sure the tike has a full belly and an empty diaper. That should ensure the little bugger stays quiet.

When the big day of your visit arrives, you'll definitely want to bring a stroller. When my son was a baby, I took him to work for a "short" visit and did not bring a stroller.

Going into work I said to myself: "Why do I need the stroller? I'm not a total pansy. He only weighs 10 pounds for God's sake."

Well, turns out, I am a total pansy. By the time that visit was over, I thought my arm was going to fall off.

To sum up, toting a baby into work is a slam dunk if you want to win people over. No one can resist cute, and nothing is cuter than a baby.

Okay, a puppy might be. What the hell, bring one of those too. Can't hurt.

Stellar Gem #70: Play "If You Leave It, They Will Come"

As a species, we're pathetic. This gem capitalizes on that for your amusement.

From time-to-time, someone will anonymously leave out something in the break room for the taking. Usually, it's food. The item might also be accompanied by a note with a message such as "Free!" or "Help yourself!"

Before we go any further, you should know that I subscribe to the "If it's free, it's for me." philosophy. For example, when faced with a plate of fresh brownies, chocolate chip cookies, or a tray of bagels with cream cheese, I feel like I've won the lottery.

Your amusement can begin once you realize people will take anything. Take produce.

We're all supposed to eat vegetables for good health, but people don't like to bring in normal, appealing looking veggies. They bring in frightening produce that looks like it was grown at Chernobyl Farms, badly misshapen and unidentifiable.

Often these farm rejects are some kind of root vegetable. A root vegetable is basically a disgusting vegetable no one wants to eat. If you are brave enough to eat it, you'll first have to cook it for a long time. Twelve hours should suffice.

On other occasions, you might stumble upon food left over from a work event, but that has been sitting out way too long unrefrigerated. I wouldn't feed it to my dog, but there it is for the worker bees to consume.

One year, all of this spawned an idea for a fun game called "If you leave it, they will come." Here's how you play:

1. Find an absurd item to give away. The more absurd the better.

2. Add the requisite sticky note proclaiming it is free for the taking.

3. Sit back, watch, and wait to see how long it takes to disappear. You won't have to wait long.

Why play this game? Because you've got nothing better to do, and it's fun.

Here are some suggestions of what you could give away: old Chinese mustard or soy sauce packets, a single salad crouton, an uncooked hamburger, a melted chocolate bar, expired dairy products, or any container of food with at least half of the contents missing. And no need to limit yourself to food items. You could also leave out any of the following: a dead flower, rusty nails, a dirty sponge, three used birthday candles, a cassette tape labeled "Rockin mix tape," a single glove, or a three-month-old lottery ticket.

Stellar Gem #71: Have a Joke Handy

Let me start by sharing a couple.

1. How do you find out who loves you more, your dog or your spouse? Lock them both in a closet for six hours. Then let them out and see which one is happy to see you.

2. For this next one, stick your index finger in the air and swirl it in small circles. Okay, now you're ready.

   Me: Knock, knock

   You: Who's there?

   Me: Woo

   You: Woo-hoo!

Hey, I like these jokes, but I'm sure you can do better.

When you have a joke to share, make sure you nail your delivery. Personally, I recommend a wry delivery.

If your timing is off, your audience is either going to respond with dead silence and blank stares, or provide you with pity laughter, which might be worse than no laughter.

By the way, if you tell someone a joke and the person responds "I don't get it," walk away. Don't try and explain it. That will only make things worse.

If you want to go dirty, have at it. I'm not opposed to dirty jokes. Funny is funny, but make sure it's funny.

Anyway, regardless of the joke, it's nice to tell them and hear them once in a while. So, maybe have one or two ready-to-go. And if this all sounds like a hassle, remember that laughter relaxes people and makes them happy. Once they let their guard down, they'll be putty in your hands. MUAHAHAHA!

Stellar Gem #72: Acquire Some Fake Vomit

My previous gem was about telling jokes. However, if you don't feel chatty, you can always pull a practical joke.

A practical joke should never inflict pain or humiliate anyone, unless you hate the person. No, I kid. It's never okay.

When choosing a practical joke, you can't go wrong with the classics, like some fake vomit, whoopee cushion, hand shocker, or the fake snake that jumps out of the phony soda can. These gags are masterpieces, like a Renoir painting or a Beethoven symphony.

Maybe you'd enjoy wrapping your cubemate's cubicle in yellow crime tape and drawing one of those dead body outlines of the floor with some chalk. Or perhaps covering all of the person's belongings in tin foil is more up your alley.

If you can't decide who to target, an ideal candidate would be anyone returning from vacation. That's because the person will be relaxed and less likely to murder you.*

Just as you don't want to severely anger anyone, you also want to avoid setting off a stampede. That means no setting off the fire alarm.

Another one to stay away from is a nutty one I remember. Someone at work secretly grabbed a co-worker's car keys. Then he moved the person's car out of sight and put the keys back where he originally found them.

The owner of the car was understandably confounded, which was funny. Quickly, however, confusion turned to panic as the person concluded that the car had been stolen. Luckily, the joker revealed himself before the police got involved.

Lastly, you probably will want to buy some supplies. Hey, don't be such a tightwad. It's a good investment.

You might want to get your supplies at Spencer's, a fine establishment that has been supplying immature idiots with these products for decades. While you're visiting the store, you can also giggle like a tween looking at the naughty merchandise.

Now get outta that chair and go play a practical joke on someone.

---

* Play a practical joke on a stressed-out person and he or she could explode like Mount Vesuvius and beat you to death with a sock full of pennies.

Stellar Gem #73: Act Childish

If you've gotten this far and are still following my advice, God help you. No, you're fine. My advice is rock solid.*

Let's be honest though. I'm proposing some childish stuff in this book. For the record, however, I don't at all see that as a bad thing.

Go spend an hour with a kid. You'll quickly be reminded that having fun comes as naturally to them as breathing. But alas, childhood is fleeting. Adulthood creeps in and crushes our youthful, carefree, fun-loving spirit. Instead of waking up anticipating fun and adventure, we drag ourselves out of bed with a sigh.

The good news is that the kid from long ago is still somewhere inside of you. Channel that inner child if you want to be happier.

Put aside the fact that the previous paragraph sounds like some serious hippie nonsense. Then think about what that looks like.

If you think like a kid, you might be able to bring some fun and games into that grim office. Unless you work at some trendy Silicon Valley company, you probably can't play laser tag, but that still leaves toys.

Even if you chase kids off your lawn while shaking your fist, I bet you can think back to your early days and remember a favorite toy. And I'm willing to bet that the thought of that toy will bring a smile to your face.

To recapture some of that childhood fun, get yourself some toys and bring them to work. Even if you won't always have time to play with them, simply seeing them will brighten your day.

If you don't know what to get, check out options online or peruse the toy aisle at Target. Nothing wrong with the classics, but if you're older with no grandkids, explore. There are bound to be fun new products you're not even aware of.

If you're a cheapo, there are always yard sales. Great bargains abound. Kids dupe parents into paying top dollar for toys. Kids get tired of the toys. Parents, desperate to declutter the house, sell them to you for pennies on the dollar.

That's why it's good to regress back to childhood, as long as there are no temper tantrums.

---

* Yes, it was hard to write that with a straight face.

Stellar Gem #74: Learn to Juggle

Juggling is another way you can keep yourself amused at work.

Think that's my dumbest idea? You grossly underestimate me. I can come up with far dumber ones.

Besides, cut me some slack. Let's see you come up with 101 unique ways to survive working for the man.

Now, pay attention. If you don't know how to juggle, you'll need to:

1. Find someone who knows how to juggle.

2. Have that person teach you how to juggle.

3. Start juggling.

If you don't know any jugglers, no worries. That's why God made YouTube. Just watch a few videos.

Who knows? With a little practice, you might become skilled at juggling.

Once you've mastered the juggling balls, you can move on to flaming torches, razor-sharp knives, and chainsaws. Maybe try juggling all three of those items simultaneously. Wouldn't that be fun? Note: Security will try and ruin your fun by lecturing you about the danger of killing yourself and/or a colleague. Pay those security killjoys no mind.

Also, if you do to start tossing about perilous objects and get hurt, you mustn't try to take legal action against me. That would hurt my feelings, and then I'd have to countersue you for being a jerk.

Now I'd like you to take a moment to ponder where your new-found hobby might lead. Nowhere is one distinct possibility. However, I can't help thinking it could open the door to a new career opportunity for you, like circus performer or children's birthday party entertainer.

Hey, don't scoff. One of the mechanics at my local garage told me once he cleans up, not as a mechanic, but as a kids' entertainer in his spare time.

I'm not an especially good juggler, although I think I could be decent with practice. I will tell you it was one way we dealt with boredom when I worked in a call center.

I realize you may still think this is an incredibly dumb idea. That's entirely possible, but it couldn't hurt to give it a try. I think you'll find it fun and maybe even gratifying once you get the hang of it.

One more tool to help on days then the time is dragging, which of course, is probably every day.

Stellar Gem #75: Find Time for a Field Trip

You carry the burden of work like a pack mule. That's why you need a break in your routine from time to time. Back in your school days, a field trip was just what the doctor ordered.

Why does that end when we jump onto the hamster wheel of full-time employment? We should carry the field trip tradition forward to the adult work world.

Let's be honest. There are times when it can all get to be too much—and our physical and mental health suffers.

Yes, some people take a periodic "mental health day." If you do, nice work. For some, however, an ad hoc day off might not be an option.

If you're worried the boss will veto a work field trip, sell it as "teambuilding" and you'll be fine. Managers find that word irresistible.

As luck would have it, literally anything can be passed off as teambuilding. A few examples: visiting a petting zoo, playing mini-golf, cow tipping, and getting hammered at a local bar. As long as you do it with co-workers, it builds priceless camaraderie and is therefore teambuilding.

One work field trip has stayed with me. I can't take credit for the idea, but someone spontaneously suggested my small group cut out and take in a mid-day movie. We had fun and we had the whole theater to ourselves.

Believe it or not, our absence for a few hours wasn't calamitous for the company. Bankruptcy was not declared. The company survived. And we enjoyed a needed break, returning to work in a better state of mind.

We're not machines and I've never understood why this is lost on so many employers. Even a cold-hearted, uncaring corporation should at least see that letting people slack a little on occasion is a wise business decision. It's not going to hurt productivity. On the contrary, it'll recharge people who then bring that extra energy back to their desks.

Once you've selected your destination and you're ready to pile into the car, I suppose you could all say "Field trip!" in unison. That seems like something people do. I think it's dorky, but I won't judge you.

Oh yea, one last tip. As was always done in school, before heading home, consider counting heads. This is especially important if your field trip involved booze. Can't have drunk Phil passed out in a ditch somewhere. If you do leave drunk Phil behind, drunk Phil will be seriously pissed next the time he sees you.

Stellar Gem #76: Make It Better with Bacon

Another way to get some respite from the grind is to go out for breakfast. Yes, breakfast. Not lunch. Everyone goes out to lunch. Breakfast mixes it up a little.

Breakfast also frequently comes with bacon and that's a giant bonus because bacon makes everything better. So, make sure you get some bacon on your plate because I can almost guarantee consuming it will make you happier. Sure, it might give you a heart attack at some point, but let's not dwell on that right now.

If you're vegetarian, knock it off. Bacon is delicious. If it helps, think of bacon as a dear friend who would be gravely insulted if you didn't order him.

As you enjoy your delicious saturated fat, please, for the love of God, abstain from talking about work. Such chit-chat will counteract the mood-enhancing effects of the bacon.

Common acceptable topics of conversation include sports, weather, movies, and music. If you want to tell everyone about your bunions or your pet goldfish, I guess that's your prerogative. No one will care, but I suspect they'll listen politely.

By the way, you shouldn't need any nudging to shy away from shop talk, especially given everyone at the table will unanimously agree it's soul crushing.

If the conversation at the table does start to drift to a corporate topic, like how the funding for Project Boring is getting cut, slam your fists on the table and shout "Hell no!" Then calmly move the conversation in a different direction.

When you finish your bacon, tell the waiter he forgot to bring it. That way you'll get more bacon.

Also, the benefits of bacon go beyond its amazing taste. Even the smell of bacon will make you happier. It smells so amazing you should rub a strip on your wrists and neck and can enjoy the aroma later when you're stuck at the office.

Viva la bacon!

Stellar Gem #77: Create a Fun Work Slogan

Boredom is a persistent problem at work, but don't despair. Instead, rely on your creativity to keep yourself amused.

The ways to have creative fun at work are almost limitless. One example: You could get together with your chums, assuming you have any, and come up with a fun work slogan.

Time spent coming up with a work slogan is an excellent way to shirk your responsibilities and enjoy a few laughs. One year a friend came up with the slogan "Where's my bourbon?" I think that was our winner that year, followed by runners up "Not this again." and "Grrr."

Once you have your new slogan, use it as much as possible. Use it when you answer the phone. Insert it into your emails. Make it your standard reply any time someone asks, "How's it going?"

If you don't want to come up with a work slogan, that's okay. I'm really just trying to encourage you to think of imaginative ways to have fun.

Some people are naturally creative, but most people have a lot of untapped creativity that's dying to come out. It stays trapped though because, for many, mundane repetitive jobs are the daily reality.

Too many employers treat their workers like robots. This is not cool. Well, it could be cool if the robots could rap and shoot deadly lasers out of their eyes. Sadly though, we're talking about boring, run-of-the-mill robots.

But you don't have to keep feeling like a boring robot. You can think of your own creative ways to make your workdays more pleasant.

Who knows? Maybe your creative ideas will spread like wildfire and make you the most popular person in the office park. If that happens, you'll be forever in my debt, so I'll be looking for you to regularly wash my car, take out my trash, clean my bathroom, etc.

Stellar Gem #78: Pump Up the Volume

It should be clear by now by now that I'm a huge proponent of escaping one's cubicle as much as possible. But tragically, escape isn't always an option.

So, what can you do to keep your sanity?

Nothing. If you haven't lost your marbles yet, it's only a matter of time.

Sorry to be blunt, but you're on the road to the nuthouse and there's no exit off that highway. All you can do is relax and enjoy the ride. Luckily, as is true with any road trip, listening to music you love makes the trip better.

It doesn't matter what kind of music you listen to. Maybe you're a polka devotee. Hey, that's cool. Cast away the shame and own it.

There are so many musical genres to enjoy . . . country, rock, classical, jazz, hip hop, on and on. I love all kinds of music and I'm grateful to live in an age where it's so accessible. Think of a song and, thanks to technology, you can be listening to that song seconds later.

It's mind-blowing how far things have evolved. I don't like to even think about all the time I wasted, first trying to find songs by dropping a needle on a record and later rewinding and fast-forwarding stupid cassette tapes.

You should be grateful too. If you lived in olden days, you'd be listening to Aunt Bessie play She'll Be Coming Around the Mountain over and over on her out-of-tune piano or trying to make music by blowing air into a moonshine jug.

It's a crying shame when people pass on music, one of life's greatest pleasures. So, make sure you pop in the ear buds once in a while. It'll do you good.

Music won't stop the onslaught of crap you have to deal with, but the right music for sure can make you happier. Plus, an added bonus: music can help block out people in your vicinity chattering when you're trying to concentrate.

Stellar Gem #79: Enjoy Websites Sans Naked People

The internet is a Godsend to those looking to slack off. Type in anything that comes to mind . . . history of squirrels, toenail collections, 14th century pants, or best Korean curse words and voilà—you have the answer to all of your questions. Yep, whatever weird stuff you're into, the internet is your best friend.

"But isn't it bad to slack off?"

No, not always. Slacking has been around since the early days of man. Back in caveman days, a Neanderthal only picked up his hunting club when the head Neanderthal was making the rounds.

Even back then, the big foreheads knew going full tilt all day was too much. Sadly, however, they didn't have internet access, which is why they had to while away the hours staring into space or at cave drawings.

Fast forward to modern times and slacking on occasion is still good for the soul, but you have to use common sense. I know. I don't like it either.

When online, as in other facets of life, being stupid seldom ends well. That's why I've come up with a few tips to help keep you out of trouble. Here they are:

1. No naked or mostly naked people, unless you work for a nudist colony or you're writing a white paper about naked people. No sexy stuff.

2. When someone is hovering, refrain from displaying a giant image of the new *[insert name of useless crap you dream of buying]*. Ditto with watching videos. Want to stream your favorite show? Great, just don't do it while anyone is looking over your shoulder.

3. Watch those keyword searches. Searching "crystal meth near me," for example, might be unwise.

I've known smart people who somehow couldn't follow these rules and got fired. You don't want to be in that club, so use your common sense.

There was a time when it was near impossible to be discreet if you wanted to read for pleasure at work. I remember people trying to discreetly read a newspaper when they were supposed to be working. They fooled no one.

By the way, if you've had the internet all your life, you're not allowed to complain. Not once have you ever had to schlep to the library on a cold, rainy night. Then try to find a book using the Dewey Decimal System and hope you brought enough dimes to make photocopies from the encyclopedia.

Stellar Gem #80: Celebrate Bogus Holidays

I don't know about you, but I find working five consecutive days from 9 a.m. to 5 p.m. uncivilized.* Survive a full week and what do you get? A measly 48 hours of freedom.

Happy employees work less. Two days a week max would be ideal. That would be very civilized.

That may not be possible but, thanks to holidays, all is not lost. The only problem—we don't observe nearly enough holidays. To remedy this, you need more paid holidays, at least three per month.

You impress me as the lazy sort, so I've done some research on your behalf—and I have excellent news. The calendar is chock full of fantastic holidays we could be celebrating, such as:

- January 23 – National Pie Day

- February 22 – International World Thinking Day

- March 31 – Bunsen Burner Day

- April 8 – Draw a Picture of a Bird Day

- May 8 – No Socks Day

- June 4 – Applesauce Cake Day

- July 22 – Rat Catcher's Day

- August 24 – Vesuvius Day

- September 16 – National Play-Doh Day

- October 25 – World Pasta Day

- November 2 – National Deviled Egg Day

- December 23 – Festivus

"But Mike, my boss will never go for this."

Okay, can we put the brakes on the negativity bro?

If the head honcho gives you any flak for taking these extra paid holidays, simply explain that each one is sacred in your religion. Then imply that you may have to speak with your team of cutthroat attorneys about discriminatory treatment.

Worst case, your boss might probe for more details about your religion. Admittedly, this could be tricky. The best course of action is to make up a religion or reference Scientology.

Now head over to your calendar and start circling all your new paid holidays.

Enjoy!

---

* On Sunday evenings, many of us spiral into a state of deep anxiety and depression at the thought of a looming, grueling solid week of toil. This is sometimes called the Sunday Night Wig Out. There are only two known cures for the wig-out, heavy drug use or distraction. Nancy Regan taught us that drugs are bad, so you should opt for distractions, like seeing a movie.

Stellar Gem #81: Act Offended

A solid education comes in handy when you're trying to navigate this crazy world. I think we can all agree on that. We can surely also agree on the basics that need to be taught in schools, like how to crack a safe or shuck an oyster.

There's one subject, however, that may not be on your list and it should. It's arguably the most critical life skill of all.

That skill is acting. Yes, you heard me. Acting.

We desperately need to teach the little scamps acting because one day they'll be all grown up and gainfully employed. When that time comes, they'll have endless opportunities to turn in an Academy Award winning performance while earning a paycheck.

How can acting help at work? Lots of ways. You could convincingly pretend to be confident in meetings, smile when the chips are down, adeptly invent excuses why you missed a deadline, or get your way by acting offended.

That's a lot, and frankly, I don't have the energy to address all of those examples, so I'll focus on my favorite—acting offended. Please don't think less of me.

Every day you're inundated with messages from co-workers. This represents a treasure trove of opportunity to get your back up.

When you get your back up, the person on the receiving end of your indignation will think twice before bothering you again, rightly concluding that you're a ticking time bomb. An added bonus is that your colleagues, eager not to provoke you, will happily go along with all of your half-baked ideas.

Now, let's walk through a few examples of how to act offended, shall we?

Example #1

Colleague: Is this the latest version of the spreadsheet?

You: How dare you question my version control! I've been creating spreadsheets since you were in diapers!

Example #2

Colleague: Nice job with that presentation today.

You: I'm sorry. Are you hitting on me? Unbelievable! You're lucky I don't call HR!

Example #3

Colleague: Would you mind setting up a meeting?

You: Hell yes, I mind! What, I don't have anything better to do than go around scheduling meetings for you?

When you finish your rant, don't forget to storm out of the room and slam the door behind you for added effect.

Stellar Gem #82: Take the Scenic Route

You hate your job for many, many, many, many, many reasons. One reason is it's monotonous.

Monotony makes work feel like the comedy classic, Groundhog Day—the brilliant movie where Bill Murray's character is forced to relive the same shitty day over and over. The movie is hilarious. The whole thing is hilarious because it's fiction. When the reality of work makes your life feel like Groundhog Day, that's not even a little bit funny.

At work, it's so easy to fall into a rut. Then we lie there in the mud, sometimes for years, because it's hard to climb out.

Economics often explains the difficulty. Unless you're lucky enough to have won the womb lottery, you probably think about money a lot and how to get more of it. That can lead anyone to settle and sometimes become accepting of a bad work situation.

But you need to make some small changes to help you break free. Something as basic as taking a different route to work could help.

Granted, if you live a block from work, your options are limited. Ditto if you depend on public transportation. If either describes you, you might as well skip ahead to my next gem.

As for the rest of you, I'm guessing you take whatever road gets you to work and back home the fastest. Makes sense, but I encourage you to try a more roundabout way. Maybe a route that's more scenic. That would be nice.*

Or, if it's viable, consider walking or biking to work. Yes, it takes longer, but it's healthy and will give you a different perspective.**

Give it a try. You might be surprised how much you enjoy it.

---

*Assumes you won't travel past crack houses, a sewage treatment plant, or a geriatric nudist colony.

**Look both ways before crossing the street. If you're on a bike or on foot and get run over by a bus, you will not feel healthier.

WAYS TO STAY HEALTHY

Your physical and mental health are important to me. (For the life of me, I don't know why I care, but I do.) And there may not be any greater risk to your health than your job.

It's one of life's cruel ironies. We say yes to jobs, in no small part, to get health insurance. Then the demands of the job tear down our health to the point of needing medical care.

I don't have an answer to fix our royally screwed up health care system. I will, however, offer some humble health-related ideas.

Don't worry. You won't need a medicine ball and I won't ask you to do any deep knee bends.

Stellar Gem #83: Abstain from Expiring at Work

Please take a moment to reflect on these lyrics from Billy Joel: "Working too hard will give you a heart attack-ack-ack-ack-ack-ack. You ought to know by now."

Very well said Billy.

Throughout human history, legions of people have held jobs that have literally killed them, often in a grisly manner. These days jobs are still killing us, but the culprit is less overt, usually stress.

The fact that I'm writing this is proof that work hasn't killed me, or at least not yet. That's no small feat considering what I've put up with since I started my first job at age 15.*

We're all going to leave this earth one day and unfortunately there are a lot of grim ways to go. One truly horrible possibility is dying at work, and that reminds me of a story.

It may or may not be true, but who cares? It gets my point across.

There once was a quiet proofreader (hard to fathom, I know) slaving away at a publishing house who expired in the middle of a shift. Yikes!

That's not even the worst part. The worst part is that no one noticed for days.

Sweet Jesus. This is my worst nightmare! I'd rather be eaten by a shark.

We mustn't allow this to happen to us. That's why, right now, we're going to take a solemn oath. We must pledge to never allow ourselves to die at work. Since we can't shake on it or pinky-swear, we'll have to rely on the honor system.

Now, if we get bitten by a vampire, this all becomes moot because we'd turn into vampires and become immortal. Everyone knows that. In case that doesn't happen, however, we have to be ready.

If the Grim Reaper pops his head into your cubicle, politely explain to him that it's a bad time and insist that he reschedule your demise, preferably in 40 years. If death refuses, make a run for it. From the looks of old Grim, I don't think he can jog, let alone run. So, you shouldn't have any trouble beating him to the door.

It's not easy knowing we'll kick the bucket one day. But we can take some solace in our pact not to buy the farm at work.

I've used up all of my death euphemisms, so you've officially come to the end of Gem #83. I trust you enjoyed it.

---

*Workers in this country put up with *a lot* of bullshit. I mean a lot. It's like living with a massive herd of bulls, each one suffering from severe case of irritable bowel syndrome.

Stellar Gem #84: Breathe Some Fresh Air

Next, let's turn our attention to something you might not think much about. No, not hygiene, and it's frankly concerning that came immediately to your mind.

What I was referring to is the air quality where you work.

If you work indoors, I doubt you'd describe the air you breathe throughout the day as fresh. On the contrary, it's likely foul, recirculated, and unhealthy.

Yep, the air you're sucking in all day may not be good for you.

It would be lovely if we could open some windows at work. But no, that's too much to hope for. The fiends who design office buildings decided we don't deserve the simple pleasure of an open window.

Granted, if we could open the windows, many would invariably jump out. And that would be disadvantageous to employers for a couple of reasons:

1. Dead employees are unproductive.

2. People falling from windows would severely damage the landscaping.

Seriously though, have you ever considered that the air you breath might be affecting how you feel? I for one think it does.

Thank God people don't smoke indoors anymore. Banning smoking in the workplace was a gigantic step in the right direction, and I'm extremely grateful I'm not inhaling second-hand smoke all day. But I still don't think we're left with good air quality.

I think we need to go outside more—at least a few times a day—to get some fresh air. Yes, I know you're busy with whatever it is you do, but it's worth it, even if you only stand outside the front door of your building.

If you're unlucky enough to work in a big, smog-ridden city, I feel for you. You'll have a harder time finding some fresh air. Hopefully you at least have a park or other green space nearby.

Wherever you choose, go there and plop down for a spell. Breath in the fresh air and you'll feel more relaxed and reenergized in no time.

Stellar Gem #85: Stand up

Who doesn't love a nice rest? When your dogs are barking, there's nothing better than parking your bum in a comfy chair.

Sometimes you straight up need a chair. Your body needs rest so you can resume frittering away your days selling waffle irons or whatever it is you do.

Here's the rub though: In the past, you might have been taking a break from doing good, old-fashioned physical exertion, like chopping wood, lifting hay bales, or wrestling an alligator. Nowadays, however, few of us engage in anything close to that during the work day.

A traditional work day might go something like this:

1. Wake up.
2. Drink coffee and shower (optional).
3. Drive to work in climate-controlled car and look for a prime parking space, which means parking as close to the front door as possible.
4. Park car and then waddle to the front door.
5. Sit down in your office chair.
6. Sit in chair for several consecutive hours.
7. Stand up.
8. Waddle back to your car.
9. Go home for the night.
10. Eat a bucket of fried chicken and a gallon of ice cream while watching bad reality TV.
11. Go to sleep.
12. Wake up and repeat.

Or, if you're lucky and work from home, you don't leave the house all day. Maybe occasionally you take a break from sitting to lie down.

Does anyone see a problem with this lifestyle?

Let's take a closer look at #6. Researchers have studied the effects of too much sitting, and their findings aren't good. It's led to sitting being labeled "the new smoking."

They found that perpetual sitting can make you seriously ill and shorten your life. Not to depress you, but they also found that working out isn't enough to counteract the damage.

What you need is a standing desk, so get one and start using it. Stand up for at least a few hours a day. If you can't swing a standing desk because your employer is too cheap and closed-minded, you have two options:

1. Get up once an hour and walk around for a few minutes. Go walk over and talk to another human or take the stairs to a bathroom on a different floor.
2. Fashion a stand-up desk for free by filling up a box so it's strong enough to hold your monitor. Maybe you have a Jack Daniels box lying around you could use.

By the way, I'm standing as I write this. I share that because I'm desperate for your approval and want you to be proud of me.

Stellar Gem #86: Don't Pull a Hammy

Working in front of a computer all day is taxing. Okay, that's an understatement. Let me rephrase. Working long hours in front of a screen is brutal.*

As highlighted in my last gem, we're spending too many hours sitting, still as a deer in a car's headlights, except for our sad little pudgy fingers typing and clicking. And we wonder why we feel horrible at the end of the day.

The human body is capable of amazing things. Running, lifting, jumping, swimming, break dancing, and Jazzercising. Yet you'll witness none of these amazing feats in your cubicle.

When you do attempt to exercise, you'll be stiff as a board and likely pull a hammy. If that happens at work, someone will call an ambulance to whisk you away to the hospital. While you're waiting for your ride writhing on the floor, co-workers will gawk and someone will probably poke you with a stick.

Is that what you want? No, I didn't think so.

A good way to avert that sad fate is to stay limber by practicing yoga. You'll reduce the risk of injury and feel less stressed. An added motivation if you're male and single: Yoga classes are full of babes, so who knows? Maybe you make a love connection and not have to keep staying home on Saturday nights playing Dungeons and Dragons.

If you suffer from acute laziness, have no fear. You can adopt my modified approach to yoga. All you need is 10 minutes or so and a desire to feel better. No sweating or difficult exertion required.

Okay, let's begin.

First, lie down on the floor.**

If you don't own a yoga mat, suck it up and stop being a wus. You don't need one.

Now, stretch whichever body parts need it most. That's it.

Note: If your body is in an extreme state of atrophy, please don't attempt to wrap your leg around your head like some sort of circus contortionist. That will land you at urgent care or the emergency room.

If you happen to pull a hammy because you failed to heed my advice, you should hang your head in shame. Then milk that injury for all its worth. It all goes back to the benefits of having other people pity you. Please refer to Gem #35 if you need a reminder on why that's important. I'm not about to repeat myself.

*If you do actual physical work for a living, the kind where you can break a sweat, you won't appreciate any of this. One day I was talking to a customer who had such a job. He was mad and told me that I didn't do any real work, that I was soft, and he bet I didn't have a single callus on my hands. I believe he was also drunk even though it was 10 a.m. and he threatened to come to Pennsylvania from Texas and beat up my boss. That gentleman was spot on. I remember checking my hands after the call and thinking, "Hmm, I'll be darned. My hands are as soft and smooth as a baby's." He never did make the trip though to open a can of whoop ass on my boss.

**If you're out of shape, you'll likely groan or grunt as you move from a standing to lying position. That's pathetic. If it makes you feel any better I'll be on my floor making similar injured animal noises.

Stellar Gem #87: Choke Down Some Salad

Rabbits love lettuce. For the life of me, I don't know why.

I mean, what's there to love? It's like eating a house plant. Rabbits don't care though. Maybe because they don't have house plants.

To a rabbit, lettuce is the perfect food. They don't even mind that it doesn't come out of the ground with flavorful salad dressing and croutons.

Anyway, I feel sorry for those rabbits. They don't know what they're missing. If they'd be open-minded for once in their lives and give a cheeseburger or slice of chocolate cake a try, I have no doubt they'd turn their cute little furry backs on lettuce forever.

Once again, I'm rambling. You're not a rabbit reading this. If you were, I'd have to no choice but to exploit you for personal financial gain.

As humans, we have to choke down salad and other veggies to stay healthy. I know, it's outrageous.

Nevertheless, we need every ounce of that nutrition to get though the slog of earning a living. As disgusting as vegetables are, the good Lord has given us some ways to make it easier to choke down lettuce and other nasty vegetables.

Take salad dressing. Maybe you've heard of it. There are different kinds. You have your ranch, your blue cheese, French, Russian, etc.* These help immensely.

Yes, I know many salad dressings are unhealthy. Maybe that counteracts the benefits. I don't know. What am I, a dietician? All I know is I can't eat lettuce without salad dressing.

Why stop at salad dressing though? You can make that lettuce even more palatable by loading it up with cheese and bacon. That will not only improve the taste, it will ensure your non-salad eating friends don't accuse you of being some kind of health nut.

This doesn't end with lettuce either. Eating other vegetables can be equally bleak, but you need to choke those down as well. At least people a lot smarter than me incessantly say we do.

Luckily, butter and salt stand at the ready to save the day like Batman and Robin. Melted cheese can also heroically save the day for certain vegetables.

All kidding aside, you can't keep living on BBQ potato chips and orange soda. That diet is going to kill you.

---

* While many countries are represented in the salad dressing aisle, I've grown bored with them. That's why I'll be launching a new line of exciting salad dressings. Keep an eye out for my delicious and savory new flavors, like Burundian, Lithuanian, and Mongolian. Yum!

Stellar Gem #88: Sit Within Three Feet of an Exit

If you have trouble getting to work on time (and who doesn't), and if you like to leave work as quickly as possible (and who doesn't)—this gem is for you.

Where you sit at work can influence your happiness. For sure, pulling up a chair next to your best chum or the office hottie will put a smile on your face, but I'm not here to talk about that. We're going to focus on sitting as close to the front door as possible. Optimally you don't want to be more than three feet from an exit.

Work/life balance is crucial to your happiness, as I'm sure your human resources department purports to support. So, it stands to reason, that the quicker you can escape and go home, the happier you'll be.

If three feet isn't viable, four feet is acceptable.

Not convinced you need to do this? Allow my friend math to explain further.

Let's say you find a new seat that gets you out the door one minute earlier. Counting lunch, you come into the building twice a day and leave the building twice a day. That's four precious minutes you'll save in a day.

I know what you thinking. Big whoop.

But over the course of a week that turns into 20 minutes, and at least 1,000 minutes a year, or 10,000 minutes over a decade. That's about 167 hours—almost 7 days!

You see, it is a big whoop after all. Seven days is a lot of precious time you could spend with family, friends, enemies, or your stuffed animals.

Since a seat near the door is very valuable, you must stop at nothing to get closer to the door. Do you hear me? Nothing!

If someone else is occupying a prime spot near the door, ask them nicely to vacate. If that doesn't work, ask yourself, "What would Tony Soprano do?"

The sooner you settle into your new digs the better. So, don't just sit there. Go find some moving boxes.

Stellar Gem #89: Don't Stab Yourself with a Pencil

It's two o'clock on a beautiful Tuesday afternoon. The flowers are in bloom, the sun is shining, and the temperature is perfect.

That's outside. You're inside.

Comatose, under bad florescent lighting, there you sit, listening to some guy in Dockers drone on about Six Sigma, synergy, or mission statements.

Then, when you're certain you can't take another minute, a disturbing thought enters your mind. Ramming your pencil into your brain suddenly begins to take on a seductive allure. That would put an end to the misery.

But hold on a second. Suicide by pencil can't be a good idea. For starters, it would hurt like hell. What's more, while I'm not a doctor, I'm certain you can't be happier if you're dead.

Luckily, there's a viable alternative to you offing yourself. Daydreaming. Daydreaming, or "zoning out" as I like to call it, is the best.

For starters, you can daydream about whatever makes you happy. For example, you can think about warm chocolate chip cookies, Tuscany, hot models—or a hot model feeding you warm chocolate chip cookies somewhere in Tuscany. The possibilities are limitless.

For the more philosophical, daydreaming offers a chance to ponder the ageless mysteries of the universe, such as:

• Is there an afterlife?

• What is the meaning of life?

• Why is life unfair?

• Aren't thin spaghetti and angel hair pasta basically the same thing?

If daydreaming doesn't appeal to you, you're too pragmatic. You likely spend all of your waking hours consumed by productive pursuits, like organizing you sock drawer and alphabetizing the condiments in your refrigerator.

Well, fear not. Zoning out will make you an even more a productive human being.

Think about it. The most valuable commodity in this world is time, right? So, why would you routinely allow others to waste your time at work?

Every time someone starts droning on about low hanging fruit, you should mentally check out because that person is wasting your time.

Use that time to figure out the important stuff, like if you should cut back on eating chocolate cake for breakfast, or start envisioning your next vacation.

Finally, if you feel it's rude to tune someone out, don't worry. Just nod once in a while and make occasional eye contact. No one will even notice your mind has drifted.

Stellar Gem #90: Don't Stab Someone Else with a Pencil

If the last gem didn't resonate, maybe you're more a proponent of ramming a pencil into someone else's skull. Before you move ahead with that plan, I want to suggest that it's another faulty way to remedy a distressing situation at work.

Consider that when Moses came down from the mountain and let everyone know thou shallest not killest one another, there was no footnote saying: "Thou may, however, rameth a pencil in thou co-worker's noggin if thouest annoyeth thee."

Was that wording left out because it would have been too difficult to carve into the stone? Hard to say; therefore, we have to play is safe and assume The Big Guy takes issue with murdering someone with a pencil.

Not to leave you high and dry, I've invested 90 seconds researching tips you easily could have found on your own. These tips should help vent some of that pent-up rage:

1. **Take a timeout.** Yes, like a three-year-old. Count to 10. If you want to make it fun, count in Swahili or count backwards and pretend you're getting ready to launch a rocket ship.

2. **Talk to a friend.** It will feel good to get whatever is bothering you off your chest. If you don't have any friends, I don't know why. You seem likeable enough. I'd offer to be your friend, but I don't have time for that.

3. **Exercise.** Hopefully you've heard of this. Vigorously move your arms and/or legs in different directions until you feel better. If your skin becomes moist, don't worry. That's called sweat. It does not require a trip to the doctor.

4. **Think, then speak.** A lot of people can't handle this one, but try. Remember, you don't have to say every thought aloud. Try running it through the filter.

5. **Figure out a solution.** Put on the big boy pants and find a peaceful way to deal with difficult people.

6. **Stay away from "I" statements.** Stop being a whiny self-centered jerk. This does not mean "You are about to be killed by a pencil." is an okay substitute for "I want to kill you with my pencil."

7. **Don't hold a grudge.** When someone pisses you off, it's logical to want to stop talking to the person, but take the high road and let it go.

8. **Laugh.** Life is absurd and you'll be dead soon enough. Whatever your ticked off about, it will pass. Humor can help that along, so stream a show that makes you chuckle.

9. **Relax.** We have different go-to ways to relax. Maybe you enjoy walking your dog, or smoking a doobie. If you relax by stabbing people, I'm not sure what to suggest.

10. **Seek professional help.** Most of us are mental. Go find a psychiatrist. Then let the doctor know you're a headcase and they'll take it from there.

If you don't like these ideas, please don't get angry—and for the love of God, put down the pencil!

Stellar Gem #91: Don't Get Stabbed by a Pencil

Wow, another gem about pencil violence?

You're right, it's too much. This is the last one, I promise.

If you don't want to be stabbed with a pencil, don't piss people off.

Saying or doing something that makes a co-worker's blood boil is a mistake. Besides being an uncool thing to do, it could trigger violence. Even if your assailant forgot to bring his 9 mm to work, chances are very good he has access to a sharpened #2 pencil.

The last thing you need is some deranged bastard chasing you around a conference table yelling expletives, so try and be nice. If that's too much to ask because you're a nasty SOB, my advice is to avoid people as much as you can.

There's no getting around it. Some people (men, if we're being honest) are walking powder kegs waiting for a spark to set an explosion off. Don't be the spark!

If you're dealing with someone with an anger management problem, maybe lay on compliments about how good they look. People can't get incensed over a compliment, or at least I don't think they can.

If pissing people off is your hobby, I'm not sure what to suggest. Maybe you could take up a new hobby, like sculpting butter or competitive eating. Or maybe get a parrot and train it to yell obscenities at people. That's a hobby you might enjoy.

Hey, call me naïve, but I think you're generally a good egg and treat people decently. It's the other eggs I'm worried about.

We should all learn to be kind or at least civil. After all, we're all imperfect people doing the best we can, stumbling along until we can kick back in retirement.

This officially concludes my pencil-related ramblings. The next time you come across a pencil at work, write poetry or do some math. No stabbing!

OUT OF THIS WORLD FREE TIME

Home and work are inextricably linked, like it or not.

What you do—or don't do—outside of work affects your mood at work and vice versa. That's why you have to find positive things to look forward to after work and on weekends.

At this point, you rightly feel deeply indebted to me for selflessly sharing so much of my sage wisdom—and I'm not finished. In my last pile of gems, we'll focus on things you should do outside of work. (Hint: The answer is not do more work.)

Before we dive in, think of yourself as a hot air balloon. Just play along. I'm trying to tee up a metaphor.

Now, when you wake up in the morning, envision your balloon filled with air. You look good, you're properly inflated, and ready to soar to new heights.

Then you go to work.

All previous tips have been designed to help you keep air in the balloon. But no advice can totally stop air from leaking out, which is why at the end of the work day you'll still feel deflated to some extent.

Once you log off, you begin a different and very important second job. You engage in activities that add air back into the balloon.

How do you do that?

Glad you asked. I have a few thoughts.

Stellar Gem #92: Help a Brother Out

Lending a hand to someone less fortunate is a solid thing to do—and it's guaranteed to make you happier.

My mom taught me that when you're in a bad mood, it's often because you're too focused on yourself. Her remedy? Help others and put their needs ahead of your own.

You won't have to look far to find someone to help. That doesn't say much for our society, but I guess it's great news if you're lazy.

"Holy hell Mike. I just gave $5 to my local guinea pig rescue. Surely that's sufficient."

No, it's not sufficient, damn it!

Giving money to a worthy cause is swell. If you have extra cash lying around; however, I'd really prefer you donate it to The Steadman Foundation.* You have my word I will have fun spending it.

Now roll up your shirt sleeves and go make a difference in someone's life. You could shovel snow for the old gov who lives down the block. If there's no snow, think of some other random act of kindness. Maybe give someone a hug, provided there's no groping.

Don't like people? I don't blame you. You, my misanthropic friend, should go help the environment or animals.

If you go the animals route, homeless dogs and cats are the obvious choices, but feel free to adopt something more exotic, like a star-nosed mole or a duck-billed platypus.

---

* No, of course you can't write off the hefty contribution to my bogus charity on your tax return. But please don't let that stop you from giving generously.

Stellar Gem #93: Consume Frosty Ale

Ben Franklin allegedly once said:

"Beer is proof that God loves us and wants us to be happy."

Did Ben really say this? What am I, a historian? I have no idea. True or not though, it's a great sentiment.

For those of you under 30 years old, you probably won't need much coaxing to go out for a beer or two (or twelve) after work. In fact, I suspect most of you are completely hammered at this very moment.

As for the rest of you, if the last happy hour you attended was during the Clinton administration, you might be overdue. Consider consuming some frosty ale at a happy hour soon, like after work today.*

Excuses to skip happy hour abound. You're trying to save money. Your bunions hurt. You have get home to watch Wheel of Fortune.

Well, I condemn your lame excuses. I can't throw a stone, however, because I've been living in a glass house stone-cold sober for a long time.

You're busy, I know. Everybody's busy. But sometimes we need to stop being busy. What you need is some good old-fashioned camaraderie mixed in with some boozing, cussing, and flirting (if you're single).

Happy hour is a good way to blow off steam, and heck, you might even find a drink that's not exorbitantly overpriced. If no one at your job can muster up the motivation to organize a happy hour, it's up to you.

Why do you look so worried? It's not terribly difficult. Simply pick a date and a local watering hole. Then send an e-mail inviting your mates to join you. That's it.

If you're a long in the tooth grump unwilling to deal with the bar scene, no problem. I get it. You might want to alternatively invite a few chums over to your house for a happy hour. Assuming you're not a jerk and you don't live 300 miles away, someone is bound to show up.

Of course, in addition to beer, when you go to the happy hour, you'll also have the opportunity to enjoy exquisite cuisine, all of which will come out of a deep frier. Yep, kick back and enjoy all the delicacies—French fries, Buffalo wings, and cheese sticks. Then on the way home you can duck into your local pharmacy for antacids.

At the end of a hard week—or maybe in the middle of one—consuming frosty ale is a perfect way to temporarily forget your troubles.

---

* Frosty ale of the non "lite" variety is my preference, but don't let me influence your beer choice. Heck, if you want to drink an Appletini or some other wussy drink, go for it.

Stellar Gem #94: Get a Canine Companion

I have a dog. Yes, it's fascinating, I know.

Dogs are amazing and you should have one. If you already do, please skip ahead.

There are many reasons to own a dog. My dog deters weirdos like you from breaking into my house, for example. Sorry, nothing personal. You just seem shady.

Disclaimer: Some dogs are ineffectual at stopping intruders. Those include all of the yippee dog breeds. Can anyone say Chihuahua?

Now, I realize you might have deliberately passed on getting a dog because dog ownership is a big responsibility. You're not wrong, but I think you can handle it.

You might also bring up the fact that dogs aren't exactly the cleanest animals, and you have a good point. For example, canines have a penchant for rolling around in poop, and even eating it sometimes.

Ugh. Sorry, let's forget that last part.

Instead, focus on all the great stuff. There is a huge upside to having a dog. Here are my top five reasons to get a dog:

1. **Loyalty.** People love to knife each other in the back. Your dog will never do that, and not because he or she can't hold a knife. Your dog will be incredibly loyal, wanting to stay physically close to you and love you unconditionally, even during times when you might not deserve it.

2. **Crazy.** When you see a crazy human coming toward you, you cross the street. Seeing a crazy (not in a vicious way) dog, on the other hand, is very funny. Crazy dog behavior can provide hours of entertainment.

3. **Adorable.** When you saunter down the street with your cute pooch, people will stop to tell you how adorable he or she is. Next thing you know you're striking up a conversation and making new friends.

4. **Happy.** Your dog will always be happy to see you. Yes, that's in no small part because of the food you'll provide, but still, pretty awesome.

5. **Loud.** Yes, barking can be annoying, but a good dog bark will scare away a burglar as well as any high-priced alarm system. Yes, I know I already mentioned this. Stop being so critical. Do you think it's easy to write a book?

We should admire dogs for another reason too—they used to work hard but they wised up. Laboring to retrieve dead birds, herd sheep, chase rats . . . screw that! Those days are long gone for most dogs. Now they lie on soft blankets, get belly rubs, and eat all day. Nice work dogs!

I hope I've coerced you into getting a dog. I really don't have an opinion on which breed you should get, although bonus points if you adopt from a shelter.

We all need more joy in our lives and a dog will deliver that to you in spades. Just imagine how nice it will be to be welcomed home after a grueling shift at work.

Stellar Gem #95: Visit the Dentist

Telling you to visit the dentist to improve your mental outlook sounds stupid, even to me.

This is why it occurred to me.

Work, as you well know, is chock full of bullshit and strife. You can't dwell on it though. Better to be grateful for any benefits your job offers. Don't take them for granted.

Take dental insurance.

There's nothing more boring than dental insurance. Well, I suppose you could argue that watching paint dry is marginally more boring.

The point is, if you're like me, you like having teeth.

Yep, teeth are darn handy. We can use them for chomping and chewing our favorite foods or we can use them to growl and snarl at our enemies. Plus, people with teeth always look sassier in photos, and you and I both know that you desperately want to look sassy.

Sure, you could let your teeth rot out of your head. Doesn't seem like a smart move to me, but by all means, have at it if that's what you want. You can always get some dentures. I personally can't get them because if I fear waking up and seeing them soaking in a glass cup on my nightstand, and that would seriously freak me out.

Wait. What's that you say? You're afraid to go to the dentist?

Oh please, suck it up.

By the way, all this dentist talk should have you thinking about how long it's been since you hopped into a dentist's chair. If you're overdue for a cleaning, schedule one soon. Once you've survived all of the scrubbing, picking, and polishing, you likely won't have to pay a dime thanks to your dental insurance.

If this doesn't make you feel grateful, ask the dentist what the bill would be if you didn't have insurance.

Yep, boring old dental insurance. Turns out it's actually pretty darn awesome. And a great reminder that there are at least a few perks extended to you by your employer.

So, be smart. Prize those pearly whites, entrust their care to a dentist, and feel good when you don't have to pay a fortune to take care of them.

Stellar Gem #96: Watch the Best Work Movie Ever

I'm now going to share a fond work memory, or more accurately, a fond not going to work memory. To give you some context, the year was 1999 and I was feeling majorly depressed about working a crappy job for crappy wages in a call center.

My fond memory has to do with the movie Office Space. As soon as I learned of this fine film, I knew I had to make haste and see it at once. Unable to wait for the weekend, I called out sick and drove to the local theater.

As you might imagine, I was virtually alone in the theater. In fact, I seem to recall that the only other patrons were a stoned looking guy and an elderly couple who looked like they'd wandered into the wrong theater.

That first viewing of Office Space was sheer bliss. I've always been a huge fan of comedies, and this movie had me falling out of my chair laughing. Naturally, I'd never allow myself to literally fall out of a movie theater chair because movie theater floors are vile and I don't want syphilis, cooties, or whatever else might be lurking down there.

Mike Judge, the creator of Office Space, is a genius, pure and simple. Office Space is brilliant, but he never got his due respect because Hollywood takes itself way too seriously. That year a movie called American Beauty won the Academy Award for Best Picture. American Beauty? Please. I hated that movie.

Office Space has also held up extremely well. The awfulness it shines a light on exists more today than ever.

Seriously, how can you not love a movie with this sort of dialogue?

- "Yeah, I just stare at my desk, but it looks like I'm working. I do that for probably another hour after lunch, too. I'd say, in a given week I probably only do about 15 minutes of real, actual, work." – *Peter*

- "There was nothing wrong with it . . . until I was about 12 years old and that no-talent ass-clown became famous and started winning Grammys." – *Michael Bolton (commenting on the singer who shares his name)*

- "I deal with the goddamn customers so the engineers don't have to. I have people skills. I am good at dealing with people. Can't you understand that? What the hell is wrong with you people?" – *Tom*

- "I was sitting in my cubicle today, and I realized, ever since I started working, every single day of my life has been worse than the day before it. So that means that every single day that you see me—that's the worst day of my life." – *Peter*

It's unfathomable to me that some people still haven't seen Office Space, but perhaps you've been in a coma. If so, I'm sorry about the coma, but now that you're up and around, please watch it soon. If you've already seen it, treat yourself and watch it again.

You'll be glad you did.

Stellar Gem #97: Hug Your Bad Habits

Don't do this. Don't do that. Eat your vegetables. No, you can't have cake for breakfast again.

I don't know about you, but I'm sick and tired of following the rules. And nowhere are there more rules than at work.

It's time to enjoy life more. You with me?

Yea, I know. Certain behaviors are bad for us. Point taken.

Nevertheless, even bad habits, in moderation, can be good honest fun and mostly harmless. That's why I want you to think of a bad habit you enjoy and embrace it.

Not sure where to begin?

Let's take carbs as an example. Somehow scrumptious bread, cookies, cake, pie, pastries, pasta, and beer are the work of the devil.

Over and over, we're told by over-zealous fitness buffs to deprive ourselves of all of the world's deliciousness so we can bounce a quarter off our abs. Unless you need a six pack because you're planning to be shirtless in a cologne ad or on the cover of a romance novel, think about it less and enjoy some carbs.

Another fine example is napping.

We live in such a sick culture, one that glorifies constantly being busy and productive. Wow, look at her. She has six jobs, seven kids, and makes her own soap. I want her life.

Hell no. That's seriously messed up and why I'm a big proponent of the siesta.

That's right, take a nap. All I ask is that you don't call it a "power nap" because that term is stupid and annoying.

When you rise from your peaceful slumber, you'll feel rejuvenated and ready to take on what remains of the day. Or maybe take the rest of the day off. Okay, let's go with that last one. It's a way better option.

Be smart though. Smoking crack is still, and always will be, a bad idea. Once you settle on a habit or two to embrace, those lifestyle changes may help you live long and prosper, just like on Star Trek. Also be sure to drop "bad" as an adjective so you're not tempted to drop the habit in a month. Now let's go eat some cake!

Stellar Gem #98: Go Away

Hey, where do you think you're going? I didn't want you to leave the room. I meant go away, as in go take a nice vacation. Tahiti perhaps. Or maybe Bayonne, New Jersey. I hear Bayonne is lovely this time of year.

Vacations are incredibly important. You know that. I know that. Yet your employer likely doesn't see it that way. That's because their #1 priority is squeezing every drop of productivity they can out of you.

Compared to other countries that don't still rely on oxen to plow fields, the U.S. is pretty darn backward. The problem is like a two-pronged fork jabbing you in the butt:

- **Prong #1.** Americans usually get shafted when it comes to paid time off. Some employers wrongly concluded that two weeks of vacation a year is adequate. Hello? Do these people own a calendar? The last time I checked there were 52 weeks in a year. Off two weeks, work fifty weeks. Please!

  Executives should spend less time worrying about stock prices and more time worrying about the welfare of their workers. And it would make good business sense because, when people have adequate time to decompress, they're happier and more productive when they return to work.

- **Prong #2.** Your mortal enemy is pretending to be our friend. Technology. You might think your phone is your best chum. If so, you're wrong.

  If the bad tech manners I called out in "Put the Dumb Smartphone Down" weren't enough, your laptop and phone make it almost impossible to unplug. It's time to scale way back and use the irreplaceable time doing something meaningful.

If you're dissatisfied with the amount of paid vacation you get, that's a legit reason to find a new gig. There are companies that give generous vacation days. Some more progressive firms even offer unlimited vacation days (and people don't abuse it). In the meantime, whatever your allotment of vacation is, use all of it.

To ensure you follow through on this, I'd like you to sign the pledge below. And, what the hell? Go get it notarized while you're at it. That will give it some added weight.

I, _____, hereby solemnly swear to take all of my hard-earned vacation days. I agree that not doing so would make me a total dummy.

_____   _____   [Notary Seal Here]
Signature   Date

Now go pack your bags and enjoy the time off!

And, yes, your idiot friends will toilet paper your cubicle while you're gone.

Stellar Gem #99: Reform Your No-good Ingrate Ways

If you're an ungrateful bastard, you should change your ways. Yes, it's easier said than done, but you gotta do it because appreciating what you have in life is key to being happier.

The big obstacle is that our good pals stress and problems love to push gratitude out of our minds. We also love to complain.

Regarding that last point, I'd like to use Thanksgiving as an example. The whole point of the holiday is to give thanks. It's right in the name for crying out loud.

Thanksgiving is also about turkey, pie, and football. No issues there. We nail those every year. However, between forkfuls and during commercials people will actually bitch and moan.

It's astounding. Settle in to "give thanks" and you might hear all kinds of dysfunctional negativity, comments like:

- "These mashed potatoes are lumpy. I wish I was dead."

- "Aunt Bertha, stop hogging all the wine!"

- "This is lame. I could be sexting my boyfriend right now."

- "This family sucks. I'm going to the mall."

Funny stuff, but still, you don't want to be one of these people. To circumvent it, you'll need to follow my 2-step gratitude program. It's very complicated, so pay close attention.

- **Step 1:** Mull over what you're grateful for. I'll start. I'm grateful for my family and friends, backscratchers (the best invention ever), and chocolate chip cookies, which I could eat every day. Beer, books, music, football, and dogs. Now you have a go at it.

- **Step 2:** Express gratitude. I prefer to do this with words, but I suppose you could also go hug someone or express your gratitude through performance art. Regardless of how you do it, it will improve your attitude about your life.

That's it. You're welcome.

Stellar Gem #100: Don't be a Financial Fuckup

Too harsh? No. This is arguably the most important gem. That's why I had to drop the F bomb—to grab your attention.

This book represents everything my wee brain could think of about how to come to terms with work and make the best of it. I hope you've found some practical wisdom amidst my rambling and attempts to make you laugh. But a book like this can't end without touching on an exit strategy from work.

Whether you dream of making goat cheese or joining a barbershop quartet, before you can quit your day job, you're going to need money—a lot of it.

For most of us, amassing the money you'll need takes decades and, sadly, most are not on track.

Saving for retirement can feel intimidating, like pushing a boulder up a hill while trying to reply to work emails. The good news is that it's not as complicated as you may have been led to believe. Stick to these basics and you'll scale that savings hill:

- If you spend more than you earn, knock it off. Chances are you're buying a lot of junk you don't need. Cut back on that spending and invest the money instead.

- Pay off that credit card debt. Paying credit card interest is for chumps. Don't be a chump.

- Save at least of 10% of your pay, more if you can.

- If your employer offers a retirement plan, don't be a schmuck (like being a chump, also something to avoid)—contribute to it.

- If that retirement plan offers company matching contributions, once again, don't be a schmuck—always contribute enough to get 100% of it.

- Like anything else, you don't want to overpay to invest. Two or three low-cost index ETFs or mutual funds will do it. Then check on it infrequently and give it a lot of time (years/decades) to grow.

Despite what advertisers have drilled into your brain your entire life, the purpose of money is not to buy happiness.* We all know deep down that's foolish. Instead, think of money as freedom, your ticket out of the rat race.

Remember the Golden Rule. He who has the gold makes the rules.

Build wealth for yourself so you can live later—on your terms. Along the way, stay positive. Progress may be slow, but don't worry. Keep at it and you'll feel happy knowing those efforts are bringing you closer and closer to emancipation.

---

* Naturally, you were extremely wise to buy this book. Money well spent, for sure. No need to start second guessing yourself. So, let's extinguish any such bad thoughts that creep into that mind of yours, like "Maybe I should return the book and get my money back." That would be a grave mistake that would haunt you for all your remaining days, and likely in the afterlife. I support whatever it takes to chase away those dark thoughts. Take a walk or play fetch with your dog. Once you've regained your sanity, we shall never speak of this again.

Stellar Gem #101: Sleep It Off

This book also wouldn't be complete if I left out catching some shut eye. Since closing our eyes is how we end our days, I've chosen to end my book with this topic. God, I'm clever.

Hey, wake up!

I know I'm boring but you need to stay awake so I can tell you about falling asleep.

Let's face it. You're not getting any younger. I mean, just look at you. Sallow skin, dark circles under your eyes . . . not pretty. I wasn't going to say anything, but as your friend I feel like I need to point out that you're a hot mess.

Don't worry though. Adequate, quality sleep will save the day. It will fill you with vim and vigor, whatever the hell they are. Plus, you'll be thinking clearer and making better decisions in no time.

I have no idea what keeps you up at night, although I imagine you dangling yarn in front of your cat to pass the time when insomnia hits. Whatever is troubling your mind, it's not worth losing sleep over. So, put away the yarn, say goodnight to kitty, and march back upstairs. You're going to bed.

Don't be ashamed of going to bed early. Sure, there are first graders who may be staying up later, but who cares? Those kids are going to bomb tomorrow's spelling bee.

Not you champ. You're going to be a well-rested winner, ready to tackle spelling challenges and whatever else life throws at you.

For many, getting into pajamas and climbing into bed is the easy part. The hard part is turning off your brain and those pesky, sleep-interfering thoughts, which are often work-related.

You've heard all of the sleep advice a million times. Stick to a good nighttime ritual, drink herbal tea, read, limit screen time, and avoid spicy enchiladas before climbing under the covers.

If none of that works, there's always drugs. Melatonin works well, or you could get something stronger from your doc.

If the drugs don't work, that's concerning. It can only mean you've done some dark, unspeakable things and your guilty conscious is keeping you up. You'll have to make that right somehow. Please go talk to a shrink. I can't handle your kind of crazy.

Talk about needing rest. This writing business has proven to be extremely taxing, so if you'll excuse me, I'm going to go lie down.

Let's Wrap This up Already

Who knew writing a book would be such a challenge? If only someone had told me what a herculean task it is, I would have devoted the time to more pragmatic tasks, like cleaning the lint out of my clothes dryer.

If you've gotten this far and hated the book, you're dead to me. No, just kidding. I'm sorry you didn't like it.

You have a gazillion ways you can spend your time. I'm humbled and flattered you spent time reading these pages.

I didn't set out to write this book. I initially began writing down things that troubled me about the 9-to-5 grind. As I starting accumulating essays, I still had no intention of publishing them as a book.

When I started thinking I might have a book, I wanted it to also be light, which is why I tried to weave in some humor. I think we all badly need more laughter in our lives, especially at work. Plus, some of my favorite authors are humorists. Dave Barry, Bill Bryson, and David Sedaris, to name a few.

I also shelved different drafts of this book for years. Part of the reason I let these pages collect dust is because I felt like wanting to publish is an egotistical pursuit. On top of that, more books are churned out in a single year than a person could read in a lifetime, but I ultimately figured it can't hurt to add one more.

There's for sure a lot of baloney between the covers of this book. I did, however, genuinely try to include what I think are some worthwhile life lessons about work. And if any of my words help you survive working for the man, I'll feel gratified.

Unfortunately, few of us can avoid the rat race and it's damn near impossible to find a job that's a well-paying consistent source of stimulation, joy, and fulfillment. (If someone tells you he or she has such a job, that person is probably drunk or delusional, or both.)

Wherever your career takes you, there will be difficult days. When you hit those rough spots, I hope you can come back to this book for a laugh and to be reminded of ways to better tolerate the nonsense. And no matter what happens at work, always savor time with family and friends and spending free time doing what you love.

Well, I guess that's about it. I wrote this book the old-fashioned way, without leaning on AI. And, truth be told, I kind of enjoyed writing it.

www.ingramcontent.com/pod-product-compliance
Lightning Source LLC
LaVergne TN
LVHW012046070526
838201LV00079B/3434